RIDING ON THE AUTISM SPECTRUM

How Horses Open New Doors
for Children with ASD

*One Teacher's Experiences Using EAAT to Instill
Confidence and Promote Independence*

Claudine Pelletier-Milet

Translated by David Walser

TRAFALGAR SQUARE
North Pomfret, Vermont

First published in 2012 by
Trafalgar Square Books
North Pomfret, Vermont 05053

Printed in the United States of America

Originally published in the French language as *Poneys et chevaux au secours de l'autisme* by Éditions Belin, Paris

Trafalgar Square Books encourages the use of approved safety helmets in all equestrian sports and activities.

Library of Congress Cataloging-in-Publication Data

Pelletier-Milet, Claudine.
[Poneys et chevaux au secours de l'autisme. English]
Riding on the autism spectrum : how working with horses and ponies opens new doors for children with ASD / Claudine Pelletier-Milet ; translated by David Walser.
    p. cm.
  Includes bibliographical references and index.
ISBN 978-1-57076-499-8 (pbk.)
1. Autism spectrum disorders in children--Treatment. 2. Horsemanship--Therapeutic use. 3. Horses--Therapeutic use. 4. Human-animal relationships. I. Title.
  RC553.A88P4513 2012
  618.92'858820651581--dc23
                          2011050044

Photos 1 and 2 courtesy of Anthony Riviere; Photos 4, 6, and 7 courtesy of David Walser; Photos 3 and 5 courtesy of Claudine Pelletier-Milet.

Book design by Lauryl Eddlemon
Cover design by RM Didier
Typefaces: Veljovic, Kabel

10 9 8 7 6 5 4 3 2 1

Contents

Important Note
From the Publisher

A utism is a general term used to describe a group of developmental disorders, often referred to as autism spectrum disorders (ASD). Symptoms typically appear in the first three years of life, and include restricted and repetitive patterns of behavior that affect an individual's ability to communicate and interact with others. It is estimated that autism affects one in every 110 births in the United States (one in 70 boys), and statistics show that the prevalence rate is significantly increasing annually.

Perhaps one of the most tragic aspects of this group of disorders is that those affected often withdraw from social engagement—they may fail to speak, respond, or make eye contact, while avoiding physical touch. It can seem as if the autistic individual is unable to "open up" to other people, or to his own emotions and feelings. This not only lays a challenging road before the person "on the autism spectrum," it causes frustration, despair, and longing on the part of parents, relatives, and friends who desperately seek reciprocation of the love and affection they cannot help but feel for the autistic child in their life.

Claudine Pelletier-Milet feels that an autistic person is someone who is, in many ways, "in the dark" and just longing to "light up." Over the last 15 years she has worked at her horseback riding stable in France, outside the mainstream debate about autism and its causes, creating a magical world in which her horses and ponies help her autistic students (her "magnificent horsemen," as she calls them) develop on their own time in a joyful and relaxed atmosphere.

When we read how Pelletier-Milet's horses open doors to the autistic individual, inviting him into the vast world that surrounds him to discover new sensations and learn to control his emotions and fears, we thought sharing her stories—originally published in the French language and with a French audience in mind—worth translating. We acknowledge that the French school of thought and related research pertaining to ASD differs in depth, perception, and terminology from that in the United States and other parts of the world. We are thankful that the United States is a world leader in advancement of ASD theory and treatment. It is even with these differences in mind that we feel Pelletier-Milet's personal experiences with autistic children, and the transformation she has witnessed time and again in the saddle, remain a universal source of inspiration and hope, and one that should be shared, regardless of native land or language.

Introduction to
Claudine Pelletier-Milet
and her work

By Catherine Mathelin-Vanier

Some of you may already know about Claudine Pelletier-Milet and the equestrian center and "pony club" she runs outside of Paris, France. In 2004, Claudine's book *Un Poney Pour Être Grand* (A pony to help growing up) described the work she does with babies on horseback. I've witnessed her "baby riders" as she calls them, and it was this that captured my interest and rooted my fascination with Claudine's techniques.

While watching these little children, some of whom were barely eighteen months old, it immediately struck me that Claudine's was no ordinary riding method. She had made her time and her ponies available to these children to help them discover a new world in which they could begin to acquire independence and a desire to communicate. Here was a technique that was helping these children not only become riders, but even more importantly, grow up.

When I took my own children to Claudine's pony club—and later on, my grandchildren—I formed a friendship with her that has grown stronger over time. Since I already had thirty years of experience of psychoanalysis in the field of young children, often those who were in some way hindered in their development, her work was of special interest to me. Our conversations covered many of the possible developments in bringing about change in the life of very young children through riding. Her "baby riders'" growing equestrian skills were apparent to all, but the evident change in their nature—the growing confidence, the newfound calm of the hyperactive, and the increased animation in those that were withdrawn—was also soon apparent.

Claudine is also trained in the field of special needs education, and she soon noticed that her methods had similarly good results when applied to children identified as "autistic" who were sent to her by care facilities and educational groups. She agreed to enroll these children in her courses: to her, every child shares the common trait of being unique, and each has different characteristics and must cope with different problems. It was clear to her that any child, whether autistic or not, could benefit from contact with her ponies.

As you read this book you will see that Claudine is not trying to make every child the same, nor is she trying to make those on the autism spectrum somehow "normal." She is simply helping each child discover the person he or she is, opening doors into our world by breaking the locks that keep them shut. She is helping autistic children discover feelings and emotions—while learning to control them—feelings that are often limited to fears, and which can prevent those with autism spectrum disorders (ASD) from moving forward.

Claudine never makes judgments in advance, whatever the diagnosis of the child that has been sent to her. She is guided by the conviction that all children are the same in these ways: they want to live and they want to be able to make contact with other people. She assumes that children on the autism spectrum share the desire, although it is stifled, to open themselves to the world. If a child cannot communicate, he will struggle to find the courage to open himself up to another person.

The success of Claudine's work with children and their parents has spurred her to investigate the reasons her methods might work, and this book, *Riding on the Autism Spectrum,* is the result of her research. She addresses the subject while providing anecdotal evidence of how equine-assisted activities and therapies (EAAT) can provide a bridge to communication. She is not presenting a "perfect" answer to the problems of autism: there probably is none.

There is so far no proof that autism is purely a genetic condition or a problem of the psyche. Autism is generally described as a combination of symptoms that hold back the child's development and thereby cut him off from the outside world. This is usually accompanied by behavioral and linguistic problems, sometimes resulting in the child being unable to speak at all. It is not considered an illness as much as it is now thought of as a "learning disability"—we do not talk about curing autistic children, but reeducating them.

Claudine's methods are based on the principle of respect, and the belief in the power of the spoken word. She tunes in to the autistic child at the stage at which she finds him and always speaks her mind, though without ever humiliating him. She helps the child to steer a course through the difficulties of life and to graduate to the next stage of his development. This does not mean that difficulties are avoided; quite the opposite, it is in overcoming them or learning to negotiate them that progress is made. Challenges are accepted and described with words, but the child is never forced to deal with them—her way is fluid and flexible, and this is reflected in how she does not mandate rigid riding techniques, either for the rider or the pony or horse.

Claudine always maintains that it is the autistic child who teaches her, not the other way round. She learns to read what the needs are of each child, then she works out her approach. Watching her at work, it is as if all her senses are concentrated on picking up the smallest signals, and then regulating her own behavior to accommodate them. She wants the child to feel that he is understood. She wants to be part of his relationship with his pony and with other people.

Claudine is highly intuitive and encourages the child to take the lead in their adventure together. For instance, when she starts working with an autistic child and he avoids eye contact, so she also avoids looking directly at him while she is speaking. When the child dislikes approaching the pony because he fears contact (when the warmth and the softness of the pony's coat frightens him), she gets around the problem by putting the child directly onto the saddle and immediately moving the pony off at a walk. As you'll read in the pages ahead, the pony's movement has a tranquilizing and comforting effect. It often requires only one or two visits to the pony club before the child has acquired an excellent seat at the walk and lets it be known how happy he is to be riding: he loses himself in the rhythmical pace of the pony and the pleasant horsey smells.

Claudine places great emphasis on the importance of these qualities: as the autistic child learns to master his sense of balance, he also learns to carry himself properly even when undergoing new experiences. She tries to instill in the child a feeling of independence and the ability to distinguish between one thing or one person and another, to accept that things and people are different. This is a difficult step for people with autism: they find it traumatic separating their own existence and that of people outside them, including the pony or horse.

Claudine has established in her work with her "baby riders" that the pony very soon becomes another living being to learn about. Even if to start with, a child thinks he is a little centaur (a combined "pony-person"), he soon learns to accept that the pony has a mind of its own and that the pony's will is only controlled by the ability of the rider; that certain movements allow the rider to persuade the pony to walk, trot, or stop. Though they do things together, the pony is clearly a separate entity. But thanks to the pony, the child can experience a feeling of greater strength and detach himself from his parents even when they are present. He understands what it is to be separated from his parents and yet not feel alone because the pony is there to support him. To enjoy this feeling of independence, the child has to learn to control his mount, and in so doing, he agrees to take a step in the educational process and accept its constraints.

Claudine's work with autistic children does, of course, take a different form to that of her work with babies, despite the similarity of the methods. Each stage in her work has to be met with huge sensitivity because autistic people feel that their very survival depends on the construction of barriers that will protect them against the world around them. Highly sensitive, they cut off all communication from the outside and provide auto stimulation in the form of repetitive, stereotypical actions that have the effect of shutting them in to an even greater degree. They avoid any form of physical contact or eye contact or even the presence of another person. There are those so paralyzed by their fear of others that it is as if they have immured themselves in a dungeon where all the openings are bolted shut. They refuse entry to everyone. They cut themselves off from any possibility of discovery or improvement in their life.

The fear and panic of these all-too-sensitive children, often of superior intelligence, is something that Claudine knows and is prepared to address. Step by small step, she persuades them to lower the drawbridge and let her enter their chaotic and terrifying castle. As the partnership takes root and they begin to have confidence in her, they allow themselves to risk embarking on a voyage to discover the world around them.

The autistic child has no sense of "being." Unable to imagine that he has a life of his own, he studiously avoids acknowledging signs of anyone else's. He seems not to be aware of feelings or interests of others. It is into this apparently "closed world" that the pony steps. At first the child clings to his rituals and the determination not to allow any change in his environment. He hides as far away as he can get: the further away are the comings and goings of ponies and people, the safer he feels. But it is difficult not to notice what is happening in the confined space of the riding school, even at a distance. At any moment his eyes can settle on other ponies, other children, and colorful objects like inflated balls, cones, and toy ducks (for example)—and these can either be in his hands or kept at a distance.

The pony, moving from place to place encourages these feelings. An autistic child will identify with the toy in his hand so that when it is removed, it feels as if he has lost his own identity. However, on the back of a pony, the rhythmical movement helps the child keep hold of the "feeling of existence" even though the objects approach and go away.

Within hearing distance of the child, Claudine speaks with spontaneity and intuition. She tries to understand what he is saying even when he is silent or having a tantrum. "The day I understood that an autistic child's scream is a cry for help was the day I saw that they are no different from young babies," Claudine explained to me. Indeed, is not all aspects of child-rearing based on this concept? A cry of displeasure provokes a response in someone nearby, perhaps to provide a bottle, a change of diaper, the comfort of physical contact, or the soon-to-be-familiar words: "You're hungry," or "You're cold, my darling." Very soon the baby learns that his cry, which seemed at first to have no meaning, evokes a response in those around him. The baby begins to understand that he exists for someone else, and they for him. The world begins to make sense.

Watching Claudine at work is to see that very early on she restarts the lines of communication that have been cut. She begins to speak and to give some sense to what the child is feeling. What's true for the child is true for the parents. Badly treated for far too long, sometimes blamed by childcare professionals, the parents of children on the autism spectrum have often suffered indescribable pain. Claudine listens to the parents; she gives them support, and allows them to see their child with different eyes. She enters the riding ring bursting with energy, vitality, and the joy of life. Because she believes that the children really want to communicate, it's not long before they do. The parents can hardly believe the progress their children are making, and in a short space of time, they are able to accept the distance that the ponies produce between them and their child. Claudine is there to help the parents as much as the children.

Claudine knows the power of words spoken honestly from the heart. She has seen their effect on the children; it is from the children and their parents that she learns what to do, just as she has learned from her own experiences. She says, "I'm giving voice to words that describe both my own thoughts and those that my autistic riders 'send' me." In fact her teaching method with the children is no different from that which she uses with her horses and ponies. "I've learned to communicate with my horses and they make an effort to accept my instruction," she explains. "I educate them as they have educated me by sending me signals that I understand. It's from this reciprocal trust that my method with my little riders has evolved."

Claudine refuses to train her horses, as she refuses to train the children, in any systematic manner. Instead she relies on a state of mutual confidence and her ability to communicate with them. It is quite remarkable to watch the pleasure the ponies show while taking part in the riding lessons. When she explains to a pony that, "Paul is very small and a little bit fearful. I want you to look after him and help him to be strong when he's with you," it seems to an outsider that the pony takes pride in "playing the game."

As it happens, Claudine has been the midwife for most of her ponies as well as caring for them and bringing them up. When they are turned out loose they will come to her as soon as they hear their name called: they are happy to obey her and to do their part. Everything unfolds as if Claudine is the "mother pony" of the herd. One day after I had been watching a riding session, a three-year-old boy asked me, "Do you think Claudine is the pony's Mommy?" Before I could answer, he added "I think she is a 'pony-lady.'" Is it perhaps this in-between state, not altogether pony or human, that allows her to get so close to the autistic children and conquer their fear?

When you finally put this book down, having finished it, you will never again write off children whom society has labeled "autistic" or "handicapped." They will become for you, as they are for her, "magnificent riders," intelligent and sensitive, waiting for us to put them in the saddle and set out alongside them on the great adventure of life.

Catherine Mathelin-Vanier
Psychoanalyst specializing in young children

Author's Note

Autism and Its Causes

Autism is a general term used to describe a group of developmental disorders, often referred to as the "autism spectrum" or "autism spectrum disorders" (ASD). It is estimated that one in every 110 babies born in the United States (one in 70 boys) are "on" the autism spectrum, and statistics show that the prevalence rate is significantly increasing annually. As prevalence rates increase, ASD already affects tens of millions of children and adults worldwide.

In the mysterious world of autism, writers have advanced different theories as to its causes. Here I shall give a brief description of some of them.

According to Catherine Mathelin-Vanier, it was Eugen Bleuler, a Swiss psychiatrist notable for his contributions to the understanding of mental illness and for coining the term *schizophrenia,* who also introduced the word *autism* in 1911 to describe the difficulties experienced by schizophrenic adults in trying to communicate. Subsequently, writers used the word "autism" to describe schizophrenic symptoms in children, but it was still not employed to describe an "illness" in its own right. It was only in 1942 that Leo Kanner, a Ukrainian child psychiatrist, took this step and called it "early developing child autism," a separate and identifiable condition—not to be confused with child psychosis.

In 1944, Hans Asperger, an Austrian pediatrician, identified another form of autism characterized by problems with socializing, performing repetitive activity, and very specific and unusual intellectual abilities. The children he described were not backward in language abilities. This subsection is now known as Asperger's Syndrome. Before 1980, there were few cases of Asperger's identified but since then, perhaps more due to diagnosis than proliferation of the condition, there has been a marked growth of them. Children that are now diagnosed as autistic were once recorded as suffering from infantile psychosis.

Françoise Livoir-Petersen, a child psychiatrist in Montpellier, France, speaks about autism in a book *La Bébés à Risque Autistique* (Babies at risk of being autistic) as being a condition that is not an illness, but one that usually shows itself in the third year of the baby's life. She explains that there is still very little definite understanding of the causes and that often the symptoms, when they emerge, are misunderstood. There are still few studies of the characteristic behavior patterns that develop during the first two years, but it is clear that there is no great consistency in them. She goes on to say that when autistic behavior emerges, it often produces difficulties in the child's family—and everyone else around him—that go from bad to worse in a spiral of incomprehension.

Françoise Dolto, a French doctor and psychoanalyst famous for her research on babies and childhood and author of many books, speaks about the lack of connection between the mental and physical aspects of an autistic child that results in the child having no sense of his own body and therefore of himself. Frances Tustin, author of the classic book, *Autistic States in Children* and many others, adds that an autistic child is the subject of premature birth in regard to his mental condition. With his undeveloped psyche, the child cannot catch up because he cannot begin to cope with what he perceives as the terrifying outer world. Donald Meltzer, psychoanalyst and author of many books including *Explorations in Autism: A Psychoanalytic Study*, explains that there is, in essence, a complete stop in the mental development of the child, whose unconscious aim is to protect himself from these terrors. Nicolas de Lahaye, a clinical psychologist, describes this cutting-off as an action that the child hopes will protect his life even though there is no further interconnection between body and mind.

We see the autistic child being unable to establish any kind of relationship or to experience sensations. As a result, he turns in on himself, has enormous difficulty in expressing his wants, and substitutes for normal behavior strange bodily gestures and tirelessly repeated actions. He can only bear completely stable environments and cannot endure change.

Throughout this book I have briefly quoted various writers: psychoanalysts, psychiatrists, psychologists, pediatricians, and other experts on autism—some of the same as those I've named on the previous pages. Their referenced work is listed in the Selected Bibliography on p. 179.

Preface

Thirty years of experience with horses in the field of equine-assisted therapy underpin this book. Every week I am sent children, adolescents, and adults to work with; in addition, I come to know the specialized organizations that send them to me, as well as the parents and families and friends. We are all part of the same team, with the same objective—to help the child, the teenager, the adult. In the process, we all learn from each other. It is a fruitful exchange.

I always take into account the parents' struggle—they frequently battle feelings of helplessness when faced with oversensitive and often highly intelligent little beings who find themselves unable to arrange their "building blocks." Like the parents, I have no firm answers, but there is something that invites me to engage in the process of reconstruction. A coherent approach by all parties concerned is essential, for then the results are extremely rewarding, as I shall demonstrate in this book.

I have received invaluable help from my friends, Catherine Mathelin-Vanier, psychoanalyst, and Nicolas de Lahaye, clinical psychologist, who say that I am able to identify with autistic people to the point that I am "at their level." I feel that the treatment of autism spectrum disorders (ASD) assumes a gulf between the person treating and the person treated. I try to eliminate that gulf and to accept that the autistic child, adolescent, or adult teaches me rather than the other way about. I agree with D.W. Winnicott—an English author, pediatrician, and psychoanalyst who was especially influential in the field of object relations theory—who says that my role is to be like a musician who does not forget his musical theory but puts it aside when he is playing.

The horse is an intermediary: it neither speaks nor passes judgment, nor does it make demands

I work even longer with my "equine students" than with my "human students." A horse is not an intrusive creature. It does not speak to you or judge you; it makes no demands. Whether because of this or despite it, the horse helps to establish connections that for unknown reasons have never been forged in people with autism. It allows "the process of rebuilding" to get underway.

You cannot judge a horse's behavior by the standards we use for humans, so in order to *understand* horses I have to *work with them.* They help me to distance myself from human reasoning. The horse is a force of nature; it is straightforward, honest, and coherent whereas a human is complex, mired in standards that he is trying to live up to, always frightened of losing control, always trying to understand and seeking reassurance, and too far removed from the problems of autism to identify with them.

If someone cannot meet my gaze, I don't look at him

The autistic child tries to protect himself from a terrifying world around him. As writes my friend Catherine Mathelin-Vanier, "He has no desire to contact this world and is blind to its approaches."

When working with children on the autism spectrum, we must not set out with the intent to understand everything they are going through or attempt to bring "the situation" under control. When I begin working with a child I try not to understand but to empathize. I don't ask questions. I just place the child in the saddle and set off at a gentle walk: the motion has a soothing effect. If he does not want to meet my eyes I don't insist. My first aim is to engender confidence.

An autistic child cuts himself off from all sensory perceptions, but the pony provides a medium through which he can discover—or rediscover— rocking, bodily contact, rhythm, as well as smells, and soon afterward, sights and sounds. When a child is born he knows nothing of the world about him but soon begins to pick up signals that build his understanding; the autistic child needs constant and continuing help to do this, but it is vitally important not to have a fixed "plan of attack." What seems to be the same behavior in two children with ASD can require a quite different approach. In spite of this difficulty, we can make real progress, as this book will, I trust, demonstrate.

Autistic children are inclined to talk and behave like automatons. They speak but there is no effort to communicate. It is vitally important not to be dragged into their world in which repetition replaces thought. I accept a state of noncomprehension, but I am on the lookout for the smallest signs of sense. I sometimes risk thinking that I understand, but I am always waiting for the children to take the lead and teach me. I try to encourage them to put their emotions into words; to be aware of pleasant sensations; to learn that some behavior patterns produce pleasant reactions from people and others produce disagreeable ones; and to be able to experience love and pleasure in human interaction.

I protect and hold the autistic person as I do my horses and ponies

My approach to autistic children is the same as my approach to horses. I soak up all the information I can without trying to organize or make sense of it.

I have witnessed so many cases of the calming effect a pony can have! For example, each year on the thirteenth of July we have a fête at the pony club. One year it began to pour with rain as we began. The guests and spectators all crowded into one-third of the main indoor riding arena, leaving the other two-thirds for the ponies and horses. The musicians perched on straw bales that line the upper level of the barn.

Faced with this apparent chaos, Steven, a five-year-old autistic child (I tell more of his story throughout this book, and in detail beginning on p. 143) started to scream. I quickly popped him in a saddle and immediately he calmed down and relaxed. This lack of organization in our surroundings also disturbed the ponies, so I caressed them and spoke to them.

I work by gentle persuasion and intuition with my horses and ponies. It comes naturally to me because I was brought up in the country and my parents were close to the land. I have always had the easiest and most natural communication with them. Similarly, horses communicate with me—the children call me "Madame Pony, the horse that speaks."

It is a big step to persuade an autistic child that a human being can also speak to him. Consider Elliot, only two-and-a-half years-old when I first met him with his mother and grandmother. One day in the riding ring with the ponies all round him, he sat down in the sand and let it run between his fingers. As a safety measure I sat down beside him and played with the sand, too. I found myself taking real pleasure in the game: it stirred a distant memory and I laughed out loud. Elliot looked up and I saw that quite unexpectedly I had established contact with him.

At first, Elliot let out cries of fear every time he discovered something new, but after a while, he relaxed and even smiled at me, as did his mother and grandmother. I was able to empathize with his fears and take them on myself, as I do with the horses.

Empathy brings me close so I am no longer a stranger

I was able to build a relationship with Elliot because I awoke something profound and strange in my own psyche; it had the effect of producing common ground between us that I felt I needed to explore. It is the same with other autistic individuals—I enter another landscape with unfamiliar trees, an older one that helps me to identify with the dark woods where the autistic person is wandering.

When I was younger I had an accident that left me in a life-threatening coma. I struggled to come out of it, and I think it may have been this experience that gave me an acute awareness of a concept of "nothingness" and separation from the normal world. I make this "other place" available to the autistic child: he can deposit his anxieties there and forget about his determination to have no contact with the outside world. It is the same thing with horses and ponies.

In this way, the child accepts all new sensations of smell, touch, sound, movement, and behavior patterns that soon become familiar and are never threatening. From these he graduates to allowing himself contact with his environment, and this in turn becomes less threatening with growing familiarity. Fears are put on a back burner; the pony, the child, and I begin to move forward together in a pleasurable way that will give birth to feelings and emotions.

Human communication is highly complex, but language, which is usually considered central to the process, often produces misunderstanding. On the other hand, messages sent without words, a form of communication that my little riders have taught me, are clear, truthful and do not lead to confusion. They are spontaneous and the child's seal is on the envelope.

By learning to interpret their nonverbal communication, I understand how each child has built a protective shell around him. Of course tenderness and vulnerability lies behind this shell, but children positively vibrate with excitement when they begin to experience emotions and sensations. They let me understand how afraid they are to abandon their protective shell, how they fear they are going to drown, how they cannot bring themselves to look people in the eye. Little by little I persuade them that they have to learn to do these things in order to climb out of their state of nothingness and to leave the dark woods.

Repetitive actions and self-mutilation cease once on horseback

Until they work with the ponies, many autistic children have sought refuge in repetitive, stereotypical behavior patterns, sometimes involving self-mutilation, which take the place of emotions. These have been like a second skin. Into this vacuum steps the pony. All at once there is contact with something that is nonthreatening, something that moves in a way that reminds the child of being carried by, or more likely inside, his mother. On horseback the repetitive behavior patterns cease; the self-harming stops. The child is anchored in the saddle without feeling trapped, and a new road opens out before him. Professor Hubert Montagner, the director of the psycho-physiology laboratory in Besançon, France, and author of several books, is right when he says that animals, such as cats and horses, allow the autistic child to unlock the doors of his world and step outside.

A horse, with its comforting motion, also absorbs the primitive fears of an autistic child, and in my training of the ponies, I encourage this awareness. Gilles Deleuze, a noted French philosopher, has written about this ability to identify with animals—my ponies and I are going to carry the child until he tells me how he wants to emerge from his prison and enter the real world.

The rocking motion of the pony as it carries the child along also has the most remarkable and beneficial effect on body posture, which automatically improves, and we can suddenly work toward the correct positioning of the body's axis (see p. 6). From then on, with the help of lots of different objects, the child begins to make sense of what he sees around him; he soon adds the awareness of shapes, textures, and sounds.

Next comes anticipation of what is about to happen: he discovers the concept of space, emotions shared with others, and the birth of thinking for himself. Pointing the finger and sharing thoughts are the first steps toward establishing a relationship with someone else, and these are followed by games of pretence and imagination.

Autistic children find it so difficult to speak, and this seems to be associated with breathing freely. Breathing out in a relaxed way is the opposite of holding everything inside oneself. Breathing is also part and parcel of speaking. Words are preceded by the act of breathing out. Here again the horse helps make the connection through his "speaking" (neighing) and his own breathing. The autistic person notices these sounds, and it is not long before words begin to appear, but only when the moment is right.

The very youngest children call me "Madame Pony," and it is because of this identification that the line of communication established with the ponies can move on to human communication—that is, *with* me. As soon as this individual contact is made, I place the child in a group where interaction with several others can occur.

My method is very much based on the child developing an image of his own body and then distinguishing what is taking place *inside* from that taking place *outside.* Sometimes it can take a year, or even two, before fears are driven back in order to allow the child to move forward, and through all these months it is the horse that comes to the rescue, providing a continuity of confidence. It takes humility to accept the fact that a horse can play the role of mediator in this process, that it can achieve things that we cannot without its help.

My work with autistic children has been greatly helped by my experience with what I call my "baby riders" (see p. 28). I use the same approach with both groups, but when I began to work with autistic children, I first read everything I could find on autism spectrum disorders and then compared the information with my own findings as I went along. I would describe the process as a continuous dialogue between horse and rider, between mind and body.

I have to show great discretion in how close to the autistic children I allow myself to get; when necessary, I have to allow them to attach themselves physically to me, but I must know the moment when I can withdraw a little, never forgetting that the end I desire is for them to be independent of me and to "stand on their own feet," mentally and emotionally. In the course of my contact with them, I encircle them physically and mentally. I allow myself to get so close to their state of mind that I feel it becomes part of me.

I have written this book to pass on the lessons that these children have taught me. I feel that many of the methods commonly used to treat autistic children bring them unnecessary distress, so therefore I have made a record of my work with autistic children, "baby riders," and my horses, as well as my thoughts, my research, and my dreams, so that perhaps we can all learn from it.

My approach is to put myself first and foremost in the shoes of the individual child I am dealing with. I "become" the autistic child if that is what helps him.

Claudine Pelletier-Milet

Part One

Exploring the Role
of Horses When Working
with Autistic Children

chapter 1

My Departure Point

*"Children can be taught little by little to accept the comforting
effect of touch. All children need this and especially autistic children."*
—Temple Grandin, Professor of Animal Science and Author of
The Way I See It: A Personal Look at Autism and Asperger's

M y theory about the autistic child, as a result of my work with
very young riders, is based on the idea that, at some point, all
development stopped as though at a particularly fragile moment,
the mechanism closed down. Parents of autistic children tell me that even
as early as three months they are aware of their child experiencing certain
difficulties, like meeting their eyes or smiling. From eight or nine months
old there are strange cries and withdrawal symptoms. Then at eighteen
months, all interaction ceases. It seems as if the poor child is dragged
inexorably down into a hellish world in which stereotypical, repeated
movements and the need to avoid any change provides some sort of protection against the outer world. A world where change is part of daily life,
and in which a child learns to recognize the difference between reality and
imagination—between others and him.

An autistic child is in one sense shut off from the outside world, but in
another way, very affected by what goes on around him. He seems capable
of receiving information that is then secreted inside without any possibility of interchange. I cannot approach these children in the same way that I

approach a normal child. I have to be keenly aware of every gesture, every indication of any reaction. We explore together the world of smells, touch, sounds, and images. I have to put myself on the same wavelength as them, but interestingly it is a slower progression than the relationship that develops between the child and the pony.

Human communication depends partly on language and thought and is plagued by misunderstandings, mistakes, and corrections. Humans have a hard time accepting differences in other people, so anyone with difficulties is not accepted easily, and this applies particularly to children in school. With the pony it is less complicated: the pony accepts the child as he is, teaches him in no time to accept contact, removes any feelings of fear, helps him to be a whole person by carrying him gently to join in the outside world he has shunned until now.

The autistic child wants to communicate but has no idea how to go about it because of his state of terror. It is as if we have to "tame" him slowly and steadily. In the process, I am constantly learning more about myself, my own prejudices, my demands on others, my wishes and intolerances. We have to try and understand more about ourselves in order to be able to understand the autistic child. A state of incomprehension in us will only add to his suffering.

The shock of being born is too much to bear

Autistic children seem to have been unable to deal with the shock of their birth. They retreat into their own protective shell where there is no light or joy. I am of the opinion that this reaction is a result of too great a sensitivity and often, a high intelligence. I do not try to invade the place where they are "hiding" as this would only produce a negative reaction. I entirely understand and respect the fact that an autistic child begins from a point at which he has a strong desire to protect himself against the "other."

Indeed I make it clear that I understand the child's fear of communicating, but thanks to the ponies, I am able to be present at the moment they are persuaded to put out a feeler. I am identified in the child's mind with the momentary feeling of security engendered by the rocking motion and contact with the pony. With calmness and serenity I build on this experience in which contact, first with an animal and then with a person outside himself, has not been terrifying.

I always include the parents

The process of opening up to the awareness of others and of the self in relation to others is composed of many steps, and I never hurry from one to the next. I also take care to include the parents and family at each stage. The pony makes the first step: I must be part of it and somehow share the moment with the parents so that we all move forward together. Any hint of anxiety would have a strong negative effect, and this applies also to the ponies. It is because of this that I work so long with them prior to including them in my program to make sure they do not exhibit stressful or aggressive characteristics. Before I allow ponies to work with autistic children I need to be confident that they are able to "absorb" the children's fears and to give them a sense of security.

The child makes contact with the pony; I am very close to the pony so I can make the transition to being in contact with the child.

My pony club is where new lines of communication are discovered

It is difficult to appreciate what a world of experience autistic children have to absorb in order to make progress in the basic abilities that we all need in order to lead useful lives. The pony with its associated smells, sights, sounds, and physical contact enables the children to start working on all these fundamental abilities: coordination; being able to distinguish between themselves and someone else; a good body posture; an appreciation of the *space around them* and the *passage of time,* besides developing awareness of *what is going on* around them; and the freeing up of the emotions. The child becomes conscious of his body, his psychic "body envelope," and the space around that defines this envelope. All this is achieved through the mediation of the pony.

The pony gives the child the chance to start again

The pony, with its once-familiar rocking movement and the fact that it "holds" the child in its safe and comforting "embrace," allows the child to regress to a primitive or archaic moment in his existence, then start forward again. The pony plays a vitally important transitional role: it mothers the child, but at the same time, is a figure of authority with rules and rituals that have to be observed.

It puts in place an intimate relationship between pony and person: by its beneficial effect on body posture in which the child's seat is anchored correctly, allowing the spine to rise up in the right position in order to carry his head, the pony allows the child to look about, to learn about space and the position of other objects and people. I became aware of the powerful effect of the pony's gentle movement by observing the effect it

Early symptoms of autism are often ignored for far too long

It is a sad fact that many children are not recognized as autistic until some time after they have displayed symptoms. My experience in dealing with baby riders (infants up to eighteen months) over a twenty-year period has given me a heightened awareness of any signs of autism, which could well be ignored or misunderstood by anxious parents, especially if they are desperately trying not to believe in the possibility of it happening to their child. Some of the signs that raise alarm signals with me are:

- Withdrawal.
- Indifference to certain sounds or a very strong reaction to them.
- Gaze focused in the distance and avoidance of eye contact: the child is inspecting his surroundings looking for places to hide in or retreat to.
- Strange body movements: turning objects round and round while they stare at them.
- Rocking back and forth and other stereotypical movements.
- Speaking little or not at all.
- Either indifference to, or apparent fascination with objects, lights, things in motion, music.
- Unnatural sensitivity to bodily contact.
- Sudden cries and shouts.

has on very young babies between a few months old and eighteen months. Very often the walking motion has the result of making them calm and attentive but the moment it stops, they often burst into tears. Such is the gift to us of these amazing creatures.

An autistic person absorbs other people's anxieties.

A normal person also absorbs the anxieties of others, particularly children, but very soon they can clear themselves of these unwelcome sensations. An autistic child finds it impossible or difficult to do so and that is why I always combine only one autistic child with a group of other child riders. When there are two children, the tendency is for each of them to take on and augment the other's anxieties. Being surrounded by children who do not have an autism spectrum disorder (ASD) and being able to observe and mimic them—thanks to the ponies—the autistic child's level of anxiety is reduced and he takes a little step toward "normality"—if only temporarily at first. The other bonus is that the other children do not think of the autistic child as being "different": they accept the child as one of them and the experience widens their own perception of normality.

My pony club is founded on the presumption of respect for all; I do not even use the word "integration" but prefer to speak about "living together." My aim is not to make the "abnormal, normal" but to make variety acceptable. The boon for the autistic children in my program is that they have something to imitate, something on which to base their behavior and, thereby, a way to start constructing a properly functioning personality. They really *need* the other children.

Anxiety in horses

Just as children absorb other people's anxieties, so do ponies. They all react differently, and it is essential to work with ones that have been trained to cope with a wide variety of situations, including those that are moderately stressful. My horses and ponies are mostly born at my farm, trained by me, and brought up to cope with children who can sometimes be difficult and demanding. They know how to carry the person, to "hold and embrace" him, to be patient, and not to react with any kind of aggressiveness.

It need hardly be said that anyone dealing with autistic children and hoping to help them must avoid all stress and anxiety. All situations have to be met with humor and good-natured reaction.

Through the medium of the ponies, we all become close

My little charges become very close to their ponies, and since I am also close to my ponies, *we all* become close. Indeed, the children begin by thinking that I am some sort of extension of the animal, but later on, I become the adult that slowly and carefully introduces them to the real world. Because of my closeness to the ponies and then to the children I feel close to the autistic state myself. I think I have a very strong awareness of the way these children understand their feelings, sensations, and the things that happen around them. I can see them taking in every detail of their new surroundings when they first arrive, rather in the manner of prey. I am the person who, with the pony's help, will guide them quietly and confidently toward accepting, rather than protecting themselves from, this new environment.

I think that my sensitivity toward their predicament is partly due to my own experience. As I related in the Introduction (see p. xviii), years ago I burst a blood vessel in my brain. I was unconscious for many days, and when I slowly climbed back into consciousness, I became aware of what "nothingness" means and the shadows that stretch across the void. My first line of communication was with my family, who gave me back my energy and my smile—and it is these that I now give to my little charges.

Françoise Dolto has written about the special intelligence of autistic children: they have their own way of looking at the world, of understanding language and of communication. It is the wrong approach to reject this as worthless, and I am often appalled at the efforts of trained workers in this field who make every effort to force change on the children in order to make them integrate, instead of adapting and changing the surroundings as much as possible to meet them in a place where they might find some familiarity.

Start treatment while the children are still young

The older the child is before he is properly treated, the more difficult it is to liberate him. I have been working with five autistic children under three years old who have all made impressive progress. At any one time I am working with up to fifteen autistic children during the week. I also support their families and build close relationships with them. I have included my experiences in this book in the hope they will be of help to others. I am greatly indebted to the families for their support, and to the children for having been my wonderful little riders.

chapter 2

The Stages of Rebuilding

"From the moment a child finds himself in new surroundings,
he enters into a relationship with them."
—Françoise Dolto and J.D. Nasio

I opened my riding school in a green paradise on the edge of a forest. Brought up in the country, I knew all about nature's caprices but, come rain or shine, I accept whatever she throws at me and live at the rhythm of my herd of horses and ponies. The place has a tangibly peaceful atmosphere that visitors often remark upon as they witness the progress made by those in difficulty.

My pony club: serenity and security

The autistic children learn that at my pony club, good can come from the "outside." Often until this day, the "outside" has to them been only a danger and threat. I recognize their fears and I have to bring them help. It is difficult to describe exactly what I bring to them but I suspect it is the beginning of their "emotional life." I have the intuitive ability to return to the point in their mental development that they have reached—and this often has little connection with their age.

And there is real and evident progress: take Elliot and Lucien, for example. People still remember Elliot prostrate in the sandpit, sifting sand through his fingers (I first spoke of him on p. xvii), and Lucien desperately clinging to his collection of objects that were indispensable to him when he first arrived. Now these same two children can sometimes be mischievous and are always exploring and active. In fact, they are not unlike other children except that they hold on to an understanding of their autistic world. I respect this difference: it enriches them. (I discuss Steven and Lucien's progress in case studies scattered throughout this book and again in more depth, in Part Two: My Journal—see p. 127.)

My aim is to share this serenity with those who need it, and it is an odd fact that, in these surroundings where animals set the pace, the difference between "normal" people and those struggling to overcome a chal-

The psychic body envelope

Autistic children shy away from physical contact as they do from any show of affection. Didier Anzieu, the distinguished French psychoanalyst known for his work on Freud's self-analysis and the concept of the psychic envelope, writes that sensations received through the skin introduce us to the complex riches of our universe even before we are born. At that point it is still not formed but it awakens the connection between what we see and of what we are conscious. It supports the idea that for us the awareness of the universe is made up of countless individual perceptions and that from this idea we can imagine there to be a psychic as well as a physical world.

The autistic child cannot grow a strong enough emotional "skin" by himself (the psychic envelope), one that will protect his inner self from the outer world: he is at the mercy of being pierced by any contact or sound. The horse or pony acts as a mediator and protects against it.

Untoward noise, like that of a delivery truck bringing hay can easily cause distress. Some children will block their ears or cry out so, in order to calm them, I take them to the source of the noise and explain what is going on. They see the tractor unloading the hay and this helps to reduce their fear.

An autistic child's envelope not only fails to protect him emotionally, but also physically. When these children first come to me they can seldom bring themselves to touch the pony's warm body, but with the saddle between them and the pony's coat, all is well.

lenge is much less evident. It is the animals that reign: autistic people get closer to animals than many other people, so the latter soon lose any feeling of superiority they might harbor.

I cannot emphasize enough the importance of the horsey smells that permeate the place. I would go as far as to say that it is the smells that make the first bridgehead for those with autism, whether very young or adult, to the outer world. The smells identify the place as they are always present and undoubtedly reassuring.

Civilized man has developed his visual and auditory abilities at the expense of the olfactory, but newborns and autistic people still have a much greater awareness of smells. They will use their sense of smell to identify a place and attach as much importance to this tag as to the visual or any sound that may have marked it. Thus, the children I work with will remember exactly where the strongest smells of horse manure are or the sweet smell of hay.

An autistic person has to feel this sense of security before he can start drawing on elements from the world about him that will enable him to build up his psychic body envelope (see sidebar, p. 12). I speak of very young children and of adults. My work embraces both these categories: each has its own structure and its own space. My pony club provides this security: the autistic child feels at ease here very quickly and never feels that he is a prisoner—I regret to say, he may feel like one in some programs and institutions dedicated to helping him.

Olivier

Olivier has been riding since he was ten years old and has mastered its different aspects: he grooms his pony, takes care of it, understands it, and is respectful. When he reached the age of twelve, I moved him over to the adult area of my riding program. He reverted in an instant to his former self, lying prostrate in a corner and repetitively handling and turning over and over his collection of objects. However, he looked around at his new surroundings—and I did not interfere with his process of growing accustomed to them—before he agreed to move forward again. Then I explained to him that he had grown bigger and stronger and it was time to have a proper horse instead of a little pony. After a while he accepted the new arrangements, became aware that the children's ring was adjacent and went to visit it. I gave him a mare, Citronelle, which he brought into the new ring for adults.

This was an important stage in Olivier's development. Autistic children are hypersensitive and interpret anything unfamiliar as intrusive. As they become more confident however, they gradually learn to accept new surroundings and challenges, but if this process is in any way violent or more than they can take, they regress into repetitive movements and "self-stimulation" in order to assure themselves of their existence.

The riding ring in my program is an enclosed space with clearly defined limits in which the horses provide something that is entirely stable, unthreatening, and composed of pleasant rituals that help to achieve this difficult transition.

The riding activities begin with smells and contact, subsequently taking on visual and auditory impressions. As soon as I think the moment is right, I talk about what is happening and put into words what I think is going on in their mind. We take stock together of the place we are in, the objects that are scattered about, and the actions we perform. We notice the noises that surround us and mark where they come from. For instance, we notice a pony neighing and we look at it together; a tractor passes by with a load of hay for the horses so we follow it with our eyes—and our ears—or we might even remark on the smell of the exhaust.

The familiarity and confidence inspired by sitting securely in the saddle on a well-trained horse or pony is another fundamental element in providing the autistic child with a feeling of security so strong that he can open his defences against the "outside" world. I think that the normal reaction of an autistic child to the world around him is a primitive one of self-preservation and that the quality of this instinct is close to that of horses. This is perhaps the reason that communication is so easily forged between the child and the pony. The pony understands and absorbs the child's anxiety; the child responds by adopting very quickly a good seat and showing the pony that he is at ease. I find this is a spontaneous form of communication that takes place without any verbal instruction and quickly extends the autistic child's area that he so jealously protects to include the pony.

My object is first of all to push out the internal carapace of self-protection to include the pony and then further to the confines of the riding school, before risking the final assault on the outside world. Autistic people are reluctant to relinquish their area of security, so each stage in their progress has to be lived through with patience. The pony with its endless patience and understanding is the perfect ally.

Physical contact with the pony teaches acceptance of contact with others

By having to be in contact with the child and, of necessity, "containing" him when in the saddle, the pony is thought to be the receptacle for elements in the psychic development of the child that have never been assimilated by him, for instance, the fears of primitive origin that prevent him from accepting physical contact. I cannot do this because the child will not usually accept contact with me when he first arrives. I do not make any effort to force contact, but the child cannot help being in contact with the pony even with the saddle as a "barrier" of sorts.

At first, the saddle may prevent actual *physical* contact with the pony, but there can be no avoiding the pony's movement, and soon the child's ankles and lower legs will inevitably touch the pony's sides; resistance eventually crumbles.

Then there are the other sensations that are unavoidable: smell, sound, and the sight of the powerful being capable of carrying the child along, dictating his body motion, posture, and position. The autistic child's consciousness is the receptacle of all these physical and sensory experiences. He has had to make sense of them, act on them, and react to them, demonstrating new skills to himself and to others.

George and Ernest

George now grooms and prepares his pony for riding. He has achieved my first two aims, and he is even coming to the aid of other human beings. When the session is over, he sweeps the pavement at the club entrance, and we have to drag him away to get him ready to leave with his family. He makes it clear that he does not want to leave.

Ernest came to the club when he was thirteen and joins in a session with other adolescents. At first he brought with him all his security objects and, in moments of stress, would seek refuge with them. Now he takes part in ball games and has carried out all the riding stages that we teach. He is a proud young man, and the club has given him such a feeling of security that he no longer brings his objects.

It might be supposed that I am recommending a secure world to which the autistic person anchors himself, but this is a dangerous way of looking at it. The safety of the riding school, with its familiar rituals, familiar smells and sounds, and physical contact with ponies and even people, is better compared to a trampoline: it is not a refuge but provides something that the autistic child or adult can rebound against. Each rebound strengthens him because it returns him to the "real world."

chapter 3

The Calming Effect of the Horse's Motion

*"Motion provided another way in which my fears were lessened.
Father often rocked me in his arms, sometimes for more than an
hour at a time. He would even eat with one hand while he continued
to rock me in his other arm. After work he would take me for
long walks in my baby carriage and sometimes in the morning
before he left for work. I would scream as soon as we stopped…
repetitive movement always had a calming effect on me."*
—Daniel Tammet, author

In his book *Born on a Blue Day*, Daniel Tammet describes his life with high-functioning autism and Savant syndrome. (His book was named "Best Book for Young Adults" in 2008 by the American Library Association.) He provides a firsthand account of the calming effect of movement when he was a child and helps us understand the effect of being carried along on the back of a pony. The child feels as if his body is "put together," and this leads to an awareness of his own identity—a sense related to that of being held together in a secure manner.

Wilfred R. Bion, an influential British psychoanalyst and author of many works on analysis, describes this security of "being held" as a structure that prevents the sensory experiences dispersing into infinite space.

Didier Houzel, a noted French child psychiatrist, adds that the protective psychic envelope (see p. 12) is something required to contain all the mental, emotional, and physical experiences, and that there is a strong desire to achieve this.

The horse is the intermediary between floating in the womb and life outside

A horse not only provides the calming effect that young children require, but because of the way it both carries and "holds" the child, it gives the autistic child a feeling that he exists. Joan Symington, best known as the author of a book on the clinical thinking of Wilfred Bion, writes that long before the baby acquires an idea of three-dimensionality or of the space inside the womb, he finds a solution to his anxiety by clinging like a sucker to whatever he can get hold of. In the same way, the autistic child attaches himself to the horse and—provided the animal is calm and secure—it will transmit the required calming effect to the child.

You could call it osmosis. It is so strong that it can even work with a child walking alongside the horse or pony rather than sitting in the saddle. I think this must be because the rhythm of the horse's walk is similar to the mother's heartbeat, thus the child remembers the time he was in the womb. It could also be that the pace of the horse reminds the child of being carried in the womb when his mother was walking. I have observed the gentle, rhythmic, rocking motion of mothers in an advanced state of pregnancy as they walk alongside an existing child on horseback.

Frances Tustin, author, and the pioneering psychotherapist renowned for her work with children with autism, maintains that the mental development and growth of the psyche of an autistic child stops at the moment of birth, when the child realizes that his body has become separate from his mother, and he simply cannot bear the idea.

My philosophy stems from the belief that the pony makes a connection with memories that go back as far as the fetal stage. This is essential because the growth of the psyche has stopped at a very rudimentary stage, and so one has to begin by going even further back, before the terror of separation from the mother made the child turn in on himself.

Bernard Golse, a French pediatrician and child psychiatrist, talks of the passage between the life in the womb and that outside. The mental life of the fetus is still clothed in mystery, but it seems that the transition from in, to out, goes hand in hand with an urge to organize and contain the myriad sensory experiences taking place.

Steven

Ever since Steven was born he could not bear to see his mother leave the room. He had never made the essential step between a weightless existence in the womb to a weighted one outside it.

The rocking motion

The pony feeds autistic children, from the first moment they are in the saddle, with a feeling of security. The rocking motion of the pony's movement returns them to a primitive moment in their existence, when they were still being carried in their mother's womb, and starts the continuum that had never got underway—that of accepting and then seeking sensations to integrate into their being. The motion echoes what is still a dim memory.

Until this moment autistic children often have not had any sense of who they are or how to differentiate themselves from their surroundings or from other people. Now they become one with the pony—and by extension, with me. Often at this point they find it necessary to touch parts of my body in the same way that they have made contact with the pony. It seems to be a necessary stage in building the image of their own selves and allowing external sensations to enter this new envelope, to nourish it, and to find their proper place and weight with the framework.

It is an exciting process, both for them and for me. They rely on me at every step, and this leaves no room for relaxation, but the rewards are great. I have learned to enter their enigmatic personal world that causes them to react to situations in unexpected ways, and when we begin to make progress, the stolen look or fleeting touch fills me with joy. And it is a joy that we both share.

An autistic child desperately wants to return to the safety of the mother's womb, but since this is impossible, he constructs a protective shell into which he can hide and reject outside sensations. The mother, at the same time, is deprived of being the receptacle of the child's emotions and day-to-day experiences, both visual and mental. Usually this is part of the bonding between child and mother. She provides a safe home, a passive container for the child's development.

The pony breaks into this secret world: the gentle movement takes the child back to safer times and the contact of the saddle reminds him of the time when he was able to hold on tightly to some part of his mother. I say the "saddle" because very often an autistic child cannot bear touching the soft warm coat of the pony. I avoid this by lifting the child directly into the saddle—without so much as looking at him, let alone talking to him. I wait for him to make the first overture.

I was sent seven young children for one day a week by a clinic's day-care center, and these children took part in a riding session. The clinic's caregiver was so impressed by the progress they made that she decided to set up a similar organization closer to where they were.

Later, one of the teachers telephoned me to say they were having trouble with a child who had shown no signs of agitation when he was with me. As with other riders, she told him that he must brush his pony. The child didn't want to and sat withdrawn in a sandpit, running the sand through his fingers. I told her to skip the grooming stage and place the child directly onto the saddle. She phoned back to say that the problem had resolved.

Didier Anzieu, a professor and psychoanalyst, has written that when a child without autism is born, for the first few months, he exists in a psychic envelope for two: the mother encloses him and he encloses his mother. With an autistic child this intermediary stage never happens, but the pony, with its rhythmical movement, returns the child to this primitive moment in his existence. And, once the child and I start communicating, I can become part of that envelope.

One day one of my riding instructors raised her voice to stop a pony from annoying another one. A twenty-one-month-old child began to cry.

I immediately said to the child, "Catherine spoke too loudly to that pony. It made you a little frightened and you have every right to be. I shall tell Catherine to speak more gently. So let's go now and take a walk in the forest. Bye-bye, Catherine!"

It was enough to calm the child who was now no longer fearful, but it was only possible to do this because I had established a relationship with him. Without this, the autistic child buries his anxieties and they pile up. I understand his cries, and I can deal with the problems that cause them. If a relationship has not been established it is difficult to be reassuring because the autistic child will not be able to confide in you. He will hide his fears in some deep recess where you will not be able to get at them. I empathize with these children's cries, and I can see that they result from an accumulation of fears that have not been dealt with. Since the child has no means of expressing his unease and is so fearful of any contact, I have recourse to other means.

Rosella Sandri, author of *La Maman et son bébé* (Mother and baby), writes about how difficult it is for a young child to assimilate the protective and embracing role of the mother. Once he does, the child can absorb and comprehend the physical experiences that his life abounds in. These come from outside, but they produce a feeling of well-being—a state of mind that is "inside."

Once born, a baby soon understands how to integrate bodily sensations with his emotions. The problem with autistic children is that they protect themselves against physical sensations from outside. However, once in the pony's saddle, they can no longer protect themselves: they are obliged to take in the effects of the motion.

No doubt if it were an unpleasant experience they would find some way of protecting themselves, but it is the opposite: they are in a strange way embraced or contained by the pony and pervaded by a pleasant feeling that drives back the threshold of their anxieties. Moreover, an automatic process of bodily rearrangement takes place. The movement of the pony dictates certain bodily positions that are doubtless an improvement on the existing ones. This improved position increases their stability and skill in keeping their balance. Soon they have what can only be described as the sensation of building a proper body structure or "psychic body envelope," as we are calling it.

Their body, that a moment ago was a bit all over the place, starts coming together in a unified and balanced way, and when this happens, their physical ability improves and they can *feel* this improvement. It is rather like a physical/psychological conversation that is "put in place." When I can see the process beginning, I concentrate on what I call the "primary sensations": that of a good safe seat, contact with the pony, and awareness of all the smells associated with the pony club.

Christian

Christian, a forty-five-year-old, lay down as we approached him. He refused to get up or in any way help us get him into the saddle. In cases like this we simply attach a harness and lift him onto it. He was perfectly at ease with this as it avoided any human contact. From then on as soon as he arrived for a session, he went toward the harness, grasped it and handed it to me. He even seemed to enjoy this little aerial trip.

Leo

When Leo, a seven-year-old autistic child, came to my pony club for the first time, he lay prostrate in a corner and rocked incessantly. Every now and then he stole a furtive glance at his new surroundings. His pony was waiting, and with his mother's help, we put him in the saddle. As we set off, the rocking motion had an immediate effect:we watched his face relaxing and saw that he had adopted a superb postural position. Then he looked around at the colored balls and rings and soon began to play with them. By the end of the session he had accepted that there were other children at play and he became part of the group.

The pony produces sensations at the surface of the rider's body thereby establishing its limits

An autistic child is extremely sensitive but seems to have no awareness of pressure or weight on the surface of his skin. Moreover he does not register pain.

Steven

When he first came to me, Steven would, for example, knock against a thorny branch without reacting, but after two years of riding, he began to notice such sensations. The smells, textures, and shapes that he encountered during this period led to other sensory discoveries.

Once again it was the pony that helped this young rider to become aware of external information that included the limits of his own body. Tapping into the earliest moments of the child's life helps him begin dealing with outside information.

Needless to say, one has to have infinite patience: it can take a long time before the autistic child no longer has to rely on the pony's comforting rocking movement. This stage in the child's progress represents a need to accept the confines of his body and the information arriving from the outside; to become aware of his physical limits; and to "build the house" in which he will live and function.

My belief is that it is very difficult for the autistic child to build up an idea of his body's limits. He is invaded by alarming sensory information that he has to make sense of. It is only when his anxiety is calmed and controlled by the movement of the pony that he can associate this task with a pleasant feeling.

Very young autistic riders adapt easily to every movement of the horse

Usually, a child without autism does not have difficulty with balancing in the saddle until about the age of six or seven, after which balance has to be relearned. Paradoxically, an autistic person of any age, who may have considerable difficulty balancing when on foot, has no problem in the saddle.

An autistic person never loses the ability to balance in the saddle (in my experience). This ability astonishes people who have not experienced it, but there is an explanation.

The vestibulocochlear nerve is developed at the fetal stage and allows the child in the womb to maneuver himself and change position. Outside influences gradually change and develop, and even impair this primitive ability. Through the contact with the pony, the autistic child is reconnected with this sense of balance that he had at a very early stage of his existence, and therefore, he has none of the problems that a child without autism and over a certain age would experience. This explains why the

Finding joy in motion and beauty

I find that when my autistic children have gone through a period of adapting to life at the pony club, they make a big leap in their riding ability. I soon get them to master the walk, trot, and canter—and the children can do them really well, with a lightness of seat and ready balance in all the paces. Instead of being unhappy with their body, they find themselves enjoying the experience—probably for the first time—of finding they can operate efficiently and show skill at what they are doing: they can make use of objects and people to help them master their chaotic inner life, so often filled with imaginary monsters.

Once their body posture has been rectified—and this happens quickly once they are in the saddle—they stop exhibiting awkward limb movements and become finely balanced, and therefore more efficient in whatever they are undertaking.

My impression is that since autistic children are soon at ease with the riding experience and because of the way their limbs begin to operate, they have a high awareness of the stimuli produced within their body, especially those relating to position and movement. One can almost see the change taking place between their improved posture and their emotional development.

It has also occurred to me that these autistic children have a heightened awareness of beauty: they watch the horses and ponies resting and playing in the paddock with obvious pleasure. They derive tremendous and evident pleasure from their mount's different paces, and these pleasurable sensations must lead to a greater self-awareness.

autistic child may well have problems on foot, often walking on the tips of his toes and disliking any change in terrain, whereas on horseback he accepts going up or downhill. On foot he is not connecting with that early stage of his existence.

Autistic children find it easy to mount, touching their saddles lightly before sinking into them. At the outset they will generally not accept stirrups but gradually come round to them and are happy applying pressure at the trot. They do this with sensitivity and achieve an impressive rising trot. Even the youngest autistic children have no problem in adapting themselves to all the horse's movements. This demonstrates that their proprioceptive and physical abilities are all present and in place but dormant until they begin riding, at which point they blossom. The pony liberates this potential.

Alexandra and Gabriel

Alexandra, whom I first came across at the clinic's daycare, sat down or even lay stretched out, as soon as we reached any kind of downhill. Gabriel, another child I met there, had an equal fear of walking uphill. But, as soon as they came to my pony club and were placed in the saddle, they had no further problems walking over uneven ground.

Nina

Nina, a, thirty-five-year-old woman with autism, would not use stirrups but hung her legs straight down the horse's flanks and coped with all the variations in terrain by using her seat. This is another example that demonstrates the cessation of development at the fetal stage.

An autistic child is unable to receive and process the continuous stream of information coming in from outside. He is unable to reach the stage of being able to interact with this flow. The sensory structure that would enable this is still not in place.

Lucien

Lucien began riding with me at the age of two-and-a-half. At the time he came he had to be pushed about in his stroller all the time, but when he discovered the pony's movement, he was perfectly content. Ever since he was born he had been terrified of the outside world and so hidden himself behind his internal feelings. The experience of being carried, held, and rocked by the pony allowed him to return to the moment when the blockage occurred and to make a new start.

Steven

Like Lucien, Steven also came to the center at the age of two-and-a-half. He had already seen me a number of times when I fetched my children from his grandmother, who, at the time, was their nanny. He gave me a furtive glance on arrival, as well as the ponies that seemed to be welcoming him. I returned his look just long enough not to frighten him and, in fact, I was rather surprised by the spontaneity of his action. I decided as always to let myself be guided by him.

I turned my attention to the pony: Praline was waiting, and with Steven watching, I put on her halter. When I approached him he put out his little hand, lightly touched Praline's coat and then sharply retracted it as though he has been burned. His mother was amazed as at home he had never caressed the dog. I saddled up Praline, asked his mother to lift him onto the saddle and put on his helmet, which he resisted half-heartedly, and we set off.

The effect was magical. Steven was soon at ease and as we took a walk in the adjacent woods he looked about at the trees. His parents tell me that he likes woods and his father takes him there whenever he can. I pointed to the trees and said, "There are the woods, Steven." He looked in the direction I was pointing and babbled like a one-year-old child. I pointed to the pony, repeating the word "pony" several times, to which Steven managed to say "ny." Half-an-hour later, he suddenly put his hands over his ears, and I understood that he had had enough, so I let him dismount, and in the process he leaned on me. I supported him and felt pleased that he had lasted so long in the first session.

Then unfortunately, it all went wrong: on the way back Steven ran off, had to be chased by his mother and then restrained in case he ran away again.

In an unfenced area, children are inclined to run away

When autistic children are not in a confined space, they often run off and can get into danger. When I was designing my riding facility I insisted on the spaces being enclosed so that we avoid this problem but, of course, when we go off into the woods, there is always a risk that the children will take off.

When we got back to the club, Steven was happy to mount the pony again, and I left him to it while I talked to his mother, who was surprised that he had made such good progress on the first day. We watched him as he discovered the big balloons and play balls, which he delighted in. His riding position was very good: his body followed the pony's smallest movement.

I explained to Steven's mother that this is the way with autistic children. I told her how it is that they are unable to throw off their anxieties that are absorbed and that build up inside them until there is no room left for pleasure and relaxation. Human intervention risks aggravating the situation because of incomprehension; the fears are increased rather than appeased. But with a pony it is entirely different. The pony has the effect of making the child assume a perfect postural position, similar to that which he had in his weightless state in the womb, and no doubt, it is this that enables him to return to that moment when he was perfectly at ease. The pony makes no demands just as the pregnant mother made none. The child is attached to an animal he trusts implicitly just as he was attached to his mother.

Riding automatically improves the child's posture

Everyone who studies the functioning of the body agrees that the springboard of movement—the foundation stone—is somewhere just forward of the base of the spine, often referred to as the perineum. The spine springs up from this area and supports the head. This point, therefore, plays an essential role in creating stability and a feeling of well-being. It also affects the expression and look of the person. This is why riders talk about the importance of a good seat.

Catherine Dolto, pediatrician and child psychologist, came to my pony club to watch a riding session with my "baby riders." At that time, I had been in the habit of only taking them after the age of eighteen months, but she suggested doing some experiments with babies as young as three or four months, long before they could sit up, let alone walk. Of course, we had the permission of the parents and held them safely in the saddle. It was astonishing to see how their little bodies appeared to unfold and adjust themselves; their expressions became concentrated and expressive.

It must be the case that the child receives the same signals from the regular motion of the pony that it received in his mother's womb. For the first time since he was born, the child can gain control of his body, begin to look around, rotate his trunk, and concentrate his gaze in the direction he wants to—all the things that a severely autistic child normally finds impossible or extremely difficult in a sitting or standing position.

It is my experience that every baby of eight or nine months automatically assumes a good posture when placed on a pony in motion. Autistic children share this gift, and the result is that their fears evaporate, and often for the first time in their lives, they have an awareness of their own body.

This process of consolidation soon leads to the child acquiring a better understanding of his surroundings. There is also the question of symmetry. An autistic person's body has, at first, more of a linear nature. The horse's motion and being "carried" helps the child to position his spine in the correct axis and to balance his right and left sides. His head is no longer fixed but relaxes so that his eyes begin to explore the world to either side. A good posture facilitates this process, and he is soon rotating and extending his field of vision to a more distant horizon.

Movement is an essential part of the awareness of self, and for an autistic child, it is often the only one: every sensory perception is linked with some movement and from the first encounter, this is what the pony provides—at the same time lowering the level of anxiety.

Steven

Steven's progress was a good example of how progress brings awareness of pain. You will remember that when he first came to me he was unaware of any pressure on his skin or even of pain. We would go for rides in the woods and if he was scratched by brambles brushing against him, he seemed not to notice it. But recently we stopped in a clearing for the ponies to graze. Steven dismounted and ran about until I heard him cry out: he had been stung by a nettle and like any other child, he scratched his leg. I asked his mother if he was now conscious of pain and she confirmed that the week before he had fallen and cried because he had hurt himself. Now, she added, he pays attention to where he is going. She told me that she had another problem with him: he had been banging his head against the wall. But, since he had been coming to me twice a week, the behavior had stopped. He was much calmer and making spectacular progress, both linguistically and in his relations with other people.

Jose

Twenty years old, Jose was so agitated that the caregivers in the home where he lived would not allow him to take part in the riding therapy. I persuaded them to allow him to do so. Normally, he had to be under control all the time to avoid him running away, but as soon as he was mounted he calmed down. From time to time, I intervened to remove his hand from his mouth, and by the end of the session he actually extended his hand to me. As soon as I took it, he retracted it, but he completely stopped jamming it in his mouth. Soon he left his hand in mine for longer periods: it became a sort of game we played together.

After six months of riding therapy he came to me one day and dragged me over to the stall where his horse, Citronelle, was stabled, kicking a bale of hay into a stall on the way, I noticed. We entered Citronelle's stall and Jose exchanged a long look with the pony without saying a word or touching it. I am also a part of this privileged triangular relationship with Jose in that I can exchange looks with him and understand immediately if his expression is one of tenderness or if he is frustrated by having to wait.

When autistic people are confident enough to share their feelings with you, their expressions can exhibit great beauty and depth. Jose has changed a lot. He no longer throws his cutlery or plate around when he is eating, and his parents can even take him to a restaurant. They are proud of their riding son.

chapter 4

The Body's Axis

*"The most important thing is to give children the
confidence to pursue their dreams because this will fashion
the future of every individual."*
—Daniel Tammet

An autistic child often displays an exaggerated extension of the chest. He flings his arms backward, is unable to grasp objects with his hands, and his head lolls about. In this condition it is hardly possible to explore his surroundings, but once on horseback, he has no choice: he automatically pulls himself together and adjusts his posture and movement to that of the horse.

It is no different for riders of any age and ability: once in the saddle, you are engaged in a conversation between body and mind, yours and the horse's. It is a continuum, and you do not have the choice of opting out. This connection between body and mind that cannot be avoided helps to straighten out the body and in some measure reduce hyperextension.

Professor André Bullinger, a doctor of psychology specializing in children in Geneva and Paris, has done research on this subject, which has been of great help to me. He points out that this extension of the arms backward on both sides of the body means that there is a loss of contact between the eyes and the area in which the hands are moving. As can readily be imagined, this connection plays a vital part in the process of learning to direct and control movement.

I always use Western saddles on the ponies and horses that are dedicated to working with babies and autistic children. They are ideal for producing a good seat, particularly in that they have the effect of lightly tipping back the pelvic area. In this way the pelvis does not become "blocked": it allows easy rotation and ensures that movement initiates, as it should, from the pelvis.

Flexing, extending, and arm gestures seem to grow from the freedom it produces. The body begins to behave in a way that is new to the child. Suddenly it is under control so the child is encouraged to take some notice of what is going on around him. He sees objects appearing and disappearing from his field of vision as he moves along. As he circulates in the riding area, he sees the same objects again and so becomes aware of their permanence. From this it is only a small step to anticipating what is about to appear.

Alain

While riding, Alain touched the big yellow ball hanging about six feet off the ground above him. He repeated this a number of times and became aware that the ball was still there when he was not looking at it. He soon registered the position of all the objects in the ring, and suddenly he was playing with his surroundings: he twisted his torso to find something he was looking for; he dropped a ball into a container on the ground; and he extended himself upward on his stirrups in order to touch another ball, tethered just out of normal reach.

Most children, and people, in general, are not completely balanced in that they favor one side more than the other. In autistic children these deficiencies sometimes may be more exaggerated, and it takes patience and time to make the necessary corrections. I always start by establishing a good seat. Balance and evenness soon follow.

Julie

Julie was three. She could not walk or sit up and only supported herself when leaning to one side. She had particular difficulty in supporting her back. After only ten minutes in the saddle, I noticed her vertebrae beginning to adjust their position. Once again the pony's movement was having its effect. Her ride lasted thirty minutes without her becoming tired or losing her good posture. Afterward, her smile told all!

In order to support and consolidate the good effects of being put into a saddle, I encourage the child to flex his body, to rotate the chest, and to reach for objects that are suspended just above head level, like our big yellow balloon. Sometimes I rotate the object because it seems that babies and autistic children are calmed by the combination of rotation and movement, as in a stroller or in a car or other vehicle. I only have to rotate the big yellow balloon to stop the tears when a baby is crying. It is not long before one sees the beginnings of coordination between eyes and hands, the improved control over the body, the reduction in spasms, and the liberation of hands and arms.

Lucie and Juliette

I also give courses at my riding school to children with cerebral palsy. Lucie, for instance, came to me when she was five. The left side of her body was atrophied and she had no power to grasp anything with her left hand. As soon as she was put in the saddle her posture improved, she began to change and to make strides toward recovery.

Juliette was another example. She was only twenty-one months when she arrived and had similar problems. Session by session, she made progress and now she has no further need of a device to hold her left hand in position. Not only were the doctors surprised by the progress these children made but it is noticeable how much pleasure the children derived from the changes.

Once again I will say that such changes stem from the fact that being put into a saddle on a moving pony automatically works on the posture. Helped by exercises, this dramatic improvement in posture has a liberating effect on the body and the way in which it works with the mind. The process of education that stopped at an early stage is allowed to make a fresh start.

Lucie, described above, is a good example of this process. At first, she would not allow me to touch her atrophied hand. Then one day I noticed her stroking the pony with this hand. Her spine had assumed its correct position, her body began to recover and she was opening herself up to the world about her.

When I go with the children to the woods, I point out the mighty oaks that soar upward from their strong roots. Humans are the same except that our stability begins in the pelvic area. Once this area assumes the correct position, the tree, or the spine in our case, rises up strongly and allows the branches—the arms—to function as they were intended to.

Lucien

When I drew Lucien's attention to a soaring oak tree, he actually rose up in his stirrups for the first time as though he wanted to emulate this wonderful object of nature.

Like the other children, Lucien loves going for rides in the woods. My riding center is separated from the woods by an embankment of varying height—the children call it "the mountains," and I use it for practicing going uphill and downhill. When the children have a good safe seat, they have no difficulty in adjusting their body position to these changes in terrain. I start with a part of the embankment that is quite low and we progress to the steepest parts when they almost reach the point of being out of balance. I can see their body adjusting and learning to cope with this novel situation and they are very good at it.

I signal the bottom of the hill and the top: we look around at what has been negotiated. We gaze at the tops of the tall trees, and we dismount and scrabble about for snails, beetles, and toadstools among the dead branches and leaves. The world is starting to construct itself around their newly balanced body, and in particular around the spine.

I once carried out a study of the babies younger than sixteen months old that ride with me. At four months, I watched them twisting about to see whatever object was nearby, like balloons and balls that moved when touched. Here were the beginnings of coordination between eye and body. Then, from little baskets attached to the side panels of the riding school, they removed tennis balls and threw them on the ground. Here was coordination, sight, and the hand's ability to grasp. I introduced a pulley system so that I could lower and raise objects that the child wanted to grasp. This made them stretch.

I use similar methods with the autistic children: I have devised a game in which they take a ball—autistic children love playing with balls—from one basket and place it in another a couple of yards away. I start by doing it myself as I walk past the two containers with a young rider. He watches me, and then he does it himself. These exercises produce an awareness of the body and start putting in place the building blocks of the child's own identity. Then there is a further step: the child begins to cooperate with the others.

Steven

Steven handed a ball that he had taken out of one of the baskets to a little girl rider. Later on, he took one of her hands in his and placed the reins in it—in the correct position. This act intrigued me because Steven had difficulty holding his own reins correctly, but he knew how to instruct another person.

Discover what each child likes and dislikes

Autistic children often experience difficulty in using their hands. Before picking up any object they will consider its shape and also its texture. Whatever the shape of an object, Lucien, for instance, would only pick it up if it was made of hard plastic.

I'm always on the lookout for the children's likes and dislikes so that I can provide them with what suits them. Lucien has been with us since he was four and has made wonderful progress. He speaks well now and can recognize the name of his pony where it is written above its saddle in the tack room. He takes part in the group games and, in particular, likes the games of pretend. He is very much aware of his pony's needs and always brushes it after a session. However, he cannot abide touching the big yellow balloon when it is deflated. I have the impression he thinks his hand will be swallowed up by it.

Every autistic child has his own peculiar reactions to various sensations, and it is imperative to be aware of the particular preferences of each as soon as possible. As with horses, you need the ability to react—or to stop reacting—to any given situation. There is no absolute answer to everything that happens. You just have to be alert and anticipate, if possible, so that you can avoid any strong reaction. Any sign of aggression and an autistic child will try to return to his protective shell.

In order to start evolving he has to be given a feeling of total security.

I can provide the autistic child with this security because I have control of the environment that fulfills the conditions, as well as the method and structure employed, which even extends to the education of the ponies and horses. I present the child with the keys that he requires to begin his apprenticeship and to face up to life's challenges. He is soon aware of the fact that he can be confident both in me and in his surroundings that he can explore, take risks, enter into an interaction with others in whom he derives confidence—while inspiring them with confidence in return—whatever his handicap might be.

As this process unfolds, the child's posture and in particular his spinal column, strengthens and stretches upward. He can join in the games where we hunt for objects, exchange looks with his teachers, the other children and his parents, when they are watching. He is able to rotate his upper body for the first time and the characteristic hyperextension disappears—though it can reappear if the child gets too excited or overtired: it is a way of withdrawing from what is going on.

Ernest, whose state of hyperactivity used to stop him doing anything at all, now moves hay into his pony's stall, and I see him exchange a knowing look with the pony. Meanwhile Steven pushes the wheelbarrow and Leon takes up the big broom. Everywhere there are activities in which the children interact with other people and with their environment. They are engaging with objects they know and like, and this emphasizes the importance of surrounding them with familiar and desirable ones.

Teaching by example

Another element to mention is the need for adults to show children by example and then encourage the child to imitate, while the adult goes through the movements several times. The autistic child needs the example and help of an adult he trusts in order to gain the courage to try something for himself, and that he should do so is one of my goals.

It must be remembered that the autistic child has to return to a very early moment in his life; the journey is long and you must always be prepared to repeat a passage and only move on to something new when the lesson has been properly absorbed. It can sometimes feel like one step backward for every two steps forward. The child needs to have time to observe his last step, to absorb the progress he has made. Once, thanks to the pony, he feels more confident in his physical state and in moving from place to place, he will pay more attention to what he is seeing. He realizes how he can touch and play with familiar objects like balloons and how what he sees is part of the process.

Little steps can involve profound emotional states and turmoil, so I have to show discretion and patience at every stage. And the stages are structured. There has to be no confusion. The exercises take place in the same way and under the same conditions, and when they have been successfully learned, they produce relaxation and smiles. Of course, the children may think of me as some sort of extension of a pony, but I have to make sure this does not separate them from me: I have to be part of their world; I have to be in their "bubble."

chapter 5

The Five Senses Bring Information

"An autistic baby cuts himself off from the world and has to invent other internal and external stimuli in order to build his own world, one in which he can try to be self-sufficient. In order to do this he has to cut himself off from all sensory perceptions."
—Catherine Mathelin-Vanier

A child without autism exhibits the ability to combine and integrate a number of sensory modalities. He develops and consolidates his psychic body envelope through his sensory experiences, which in turn produce information about what is going on around him and record it in his brain. Sensory perception is, therefore, at the root of psychic development and leads to emotions and thoughts taking wing.

The sensory flow could be defined as a multitude of signals that are continuously systematized and arranged; the degree to which this succeeds in the educational process depends on the ability to concentrate and the amount of outside stimulation. A child left all day long by himself, perhaps confined to the same space, will receive less information and, therefore, absorb less than a child leading a fuller life exposed to a variety of people, places, and experiences.

An autistic child has too fragile a psychic envelope to allow anything like this to take place. He adjusts badly to every situation: either he becomes too excited or does not respond at all. He cuts himself off from this continuum, turns in on himself, and creates his own modes of conduct that are not regulated by outside influences. He is too frightened of them and by other people to allow them entry.

In the end he is so occupied with putting his defenses in place, he is starved of the sensory experiences that in normal circumstances produce continual growth. The building blocks of emotions, perceptions, and relationships with other people are missing. He does not adjust to different situations and very often his behavior is inappropriate to the circumstances at that moment. He may show signs of overstimulation, or he may be like a light turned off without any connection to what is happening.

In her book, *Thinking in Pictures and Other Reports from My Life with Autism,* Temple Grandin, a Professor at Colorado State University and best-selling author who has high-functioning autism, talks about the vital importance of physical stimulation, such as strong pressures applied to various parts of the body, as well as different textures, when trying to persuade the damaged nervous system to repair itself and to build connections. She explains that an autistic child has a preference for sensations that originate close to home. The sense of touch, taste, and smell are at first the only ones he allows. Sight and hearing are delayed for later; hence, the almost magical effect of riding.

Once in the saddle the process of absorbing and handling information begins as an automatic and nonstop concomitant of what he is doing. Touch is there from the moment he is in the saddle, and he is soon aware of the associated warm horsey smells. Then he might become conscious of the sounds of the riding arena, and because it is a confined space, he notices the same objects and people as we circulate. This familiarity breeds confidence and removes anxiety: essential elements at all stages of progress.

I am there to put the child's thoughts into words and say what is attracting his attention, and this reinforces the learning process. As I described earlier, I also use gestures—they could be described as mime— to reinforce actions and ideas. It is worth pointing out that all my introductory riding work with children and adults takes place at a walk. Only later do we go on to trot and canter, as I've mentioned, but never so soon that there could be any risk of causing anxiety. Total confidence is an absolute prerequisite; the child will make it clear to me, even if not by word of mouth, when he wants to move on to the next stage.

Hector

Hector came to me at two-and-a-half. He had severe ocular motor apraxia, a condition in which children often use head thrusts to move their eyes from left to right, producing muscular problems, showing particular difficulty with maintaining his equilibrium. For the first ten minutes in the saddle, he wobbled about without altogether losing his balance. Then he learned to regulate his movement with that of the pony and thereafter held himself up like any other child.

As with all the other children the pleasure Hector derived from riding was quite evident. These children often show a real sense of desire to advance, and these two elements are very much a part of developing new connections and circuits in the brain.

I am not saying that Hector is cured—there was, and still is, a malformation of the brain—but he went a long way to reequilibrate his balance and began to walk much better. When he came to me for the first time he couldn't even stand up. He was receiving other therapy outside my pony club and only rode, although he came regularly, during the holidays—so it is difficult to establish what made the greatest change. However, he must have ridden ten times and made swift progress—progress that had not disappeared when he came back the following spring.

Temple Grandin has said that since adults are still capable of producing new circuits, the experiences we have with children offers hope for them, as well. However, it is with children that progress is most noticeable, so as I discussed before, early diagnosis and identification of problems are vitally important.

The pony works its magic

From Day One the child finds himself absorbing sensory perceptions from his contact with the pony. At the same time I am allowed into their world. The pony stimulates them into adopting a good seat and good posture that, in turn, allows movement and observation to come into play. Hyperactivity visibly reduces and a sense of pleasure and a desire to make headway drives the learning curve. The pony and I are the vectors that allow the transmission of sensory perceptions. My aim, of course, is to establish permanent change, to put in place the building blocks that the child will have pleasure in arranging into his new self, a structure that is part of the surrounding world and not separated from it.

It need hardly be said that it is an exhausting business working with the children. At each day's end I feel I have given my all. It cannot be otherwise since the children are unable on their own to find the calm and security they need in order to receive sensory perceptions and integrate each new one in the fabric of their being—in other words, to put the building blocks together.

Whereas a normal child bonds with his mother and responds to basic needs like food and sleep, followed by a need to touch and be touched, parents of autistic children tell me that physical contact provokes tears, screams, or indifference. At the same time they appear to have a need to have their mother present. Steven for instance would burst into tears as soon as his mother left the room. Not being able to differentiate properly between his mother and himself, it was as if a part of his self left the room whenever she did. This demonstrates how sensitive he was but also that he had not at that point been able to integrate outside sensations in any meaningful way, let alone emotions, with his physical self. After his contact with the ponies, he dropped his defenses, allowing entry to new sensations and learning to put them in place.

My work with babies has been an enormous help. The autistic children, although older when they come to me, are still at a "baby stage" mentally, even when they are actually five or six years old; my familiarity and knowledge of babies and their problems has been an important part of my education.

SIGHT

Whenever we stop at some place we are inundated with information that is registered by our senses. We organize this information in the way that accords with our emotional state and our preoccupations at that time. We establish a relationship with the area, the objects that fill it, and the people that inhabit it. We store away information that will help us to relate to all this and enable us to decide what to do when something happens.

What we sense engages our physical and psychological makeup. Some situations will provoke panic and fear as well as physical reactions, such as sweating and trembling. On occasion, we feel we cannot cope or face up to these anxieties, and this reaction has some similarity to autism: we shut ourselves off, close down the hatches, and even burst into tears if the tension is more than we can bear.

Entering a new space

Temple Grandin describes how, when a "prey" animal comes into a new space, it looks all around. An autistic child also does this but with a strange characteristic: he does not move his head smoothly around, watching the surroundings appear and move slowly past, but instead his head jerks—almost imperceptibly—as he goes through the 360 degrees. Added to this, his head is usually turned upward (perhaps because mentally he is still very much a child and children have to look up at most things surrounding them).

These children have an incredible memory for the details of what they see and are disturbed by changes. Knowing this and also understanding how fearful they are, I point out any changes to them. Later on I will deliberately make changes and join in the experience of meeting them—though the children are always in a state of being comforted by the pony. Just consider the difference between a step in their learning process, such as I have described, and that of going to a doctor's office— often a terrifying event, full of unfamiliar sights, sounds, smells, and people who look at them and ask questions. They become more and more anxious until they explode.

Autistic children are closer to the animal world

Temple Grandin's comparison with a prey animal is also interesting in that autistic children are, I am certain, closer to the animal world than we are. One theory even suggests that a child's first sight of a face—usually his mother's—is taken to be the face of an aggressor. However that may be, an autistic child remains entangled in this early primitive, archaic state, and for this reason, feels much more comfortable with animals than with people.

Being only too aware of how they perceive their new surroundings, I always encourage my riders to take them in by observing, listening, touching, and smelling.

A baby born without autism establishes landmarks at a very early stage by looking. He meets his mother's eyes, often as early as three months old, becomes aware of familiar faces, and takes in his surroundings. This does not take place with autistic children, and when they first come to me, they rarely focus on any particular thing. They tend to stare at what is taking place around them with the object of avoiding any intrusion into their private world. But whereas they cannot focus on a person's eyes, they have no problem in engaging the pony's eyes. The pony is not classed as part of the surrounding threat; it makes no demands, nor does it speak, and it produces an instant feeling of comfort and security by its gently rocking motion.

The horse is not seen as making demands: it neither speaks, looks, nor asks—it rocks and comforts

Didier Houzel shares the case of Anne: the first signs of a breakdown in communication with Anne were noticed at the age of only four months when she refused any eye contact, something that normally begins to take place at this age. Babies start meeting the eye at three or four months old, sometimes earlier, but autistic children do not take this step, rarely focusing on a particular object or person close by. They favor their peripheral vision and seem to take in everything that is taking place around them but at a distance.

Arnaud

Every morning, Arnaud followed the same procedure. He carefully studied his surroundings. Sometimes his interest was held by something that we might not even have noticed, and then he waved his arms. It took several years for him to communicate with the teachers and be willing to explore.

This year the association "Reeducation by Equitation" held its jamboree (games on ponies) at my riding facility. There were eighty-three participants, but if you include the officials and relatives, there were many more.

Arnaud sat silently in his nice riding outfit, tirelessly turning over his collection of security objects, head lowered but occasionally snatching furtive looks at what was going on around him. After taking it all in, piece by piece, until he had covered the whole area (but returning regularly to move his objects), he came to where we were saddling up the participants and repeated the same careful process: working from right to left, and taking everything in, frame by frame.

I deduce from this that Arnaud is not capable of taking in a new situation in its entirety. He has to do it in a defensive way, little by little, and only then is he confident enough to participate. And participate he did! After a shaky start during which he observed everything as through a stockade, he went on to have a wonderful day: he succeeded in participating, he mingled with other people, he proudly accepted his medal and his prize.

Give the child enough time

When I take an autistic child under my wing, I observe his way of registering his surroundings. If at first he can only do this while apparently withdrawing, I do not interfere. If he just wants to sit in the sand pit and trickle the sand through his fingers, so be it. My little riders show a preference for things that run like sand, revolve like big balls, and turn like wheels.

My approach takes this into account: large, colorful balloon balls are suspended around the arena in various places and at different heights. This encourages the children to look, not only straight ahead, but upward and downward, and in front and behind them. It helps them to locate themselves in a space and to satisfy their desire to touch things by learning to move the pony where they can do this.

The importance of familiar and safe surroundings

The majority of the children seem hardly to notice either other people or items about them, but I can see their snatched glances as though they are trying to establish the boundaries and landmarks of their surroundings. Sometimes I think they appear not to be seeing enough, at other times too much, but whatever is happening, it is not long before they drop their defenses.

At my pony club the enclosed environment is very reassuring: everything has its place and function, and it does not spring surprises. This is so evident to observers that they often remark on the fact that it is not easy to tell the children with autism from those without. Autistic children have a natural riding ability with poise and balance, and a riding seat that is often better than that of my other riding students.

During a child's early development, it is thought that there are two forces at work: the first and most primitive is the visual awareness of surroundings before the child has actually focused on an object or person. This is thought to be important in that it helps the formation of physical reactions including alertness and body orientation. The second force, which comes into play a little later, appears to concern the visual cortex and explains the way a child of less than three months takes in his surroundings in snapshot form, moving from one to another. At about three months, these two forces integrate in such a way that the visual ability allows the child to place himself in his surroundings.

An autistic child has problems at this juncture: he has difficulty concentrating on a "snapshot," or for example, the eyes of another person, long enough to convert the experience into a building block—one that helps to integrate the information around him—and combine it with his own individual needs, responses, and reactions.

A child is usually able to respond to the outside world and the way in which he relates to his own being, but an autistic child cannot do this. His reactions seem to have no connection with anything apparent; they are filled with anxiety, often surprising and sometimes violent. On his own he cannot reassure himself, so he requires the presence of an understanding adult who will take the child's dilemma seriously and try to deal with it.

Luigi

One of my little riders is Luigi, a three-year-old diagnosed with depression associated with having had a wet nurse. His parents live in Paris and were able to bring him to my riding school during summer vacation. As a result of his progress, he is now brought to me every week.

Luigi's main problem seemed to be concerned with food, and he had a particular horror of tomatoes. By chance my neighbor, who has a small farm, had given me some young tomato plants that I had planted next to the arena. After each session, I took Luigi to see the tomatoes that by this time were large, red, and delicious looking. I picked one and handed it to Luigi; although he took it in his hand he began to tremble all over. He really was frightened so I took the tomato back and handed it to his mother.

The next day we went back to see the tomatoes, and I invited Luigi to pick one and give it to his mother. He got as far as picking it before dropping it like a hot potato. The next day we repeated our visit to the tomatoes, and his fear had evaporated.

I have no idea why Luigi had this fear: perhaps it was that the color red reminded him of fire? (On the other hand, I have noticed that autistic children are usually attracted to red: they prefer a red carpet to any other, they prefer a red helmet, and they choose red balls to play with, whereas my other students will usually choose a softer color like yellow.) Whatever the reason, Luigi now happily eats tomatoes. He trusted me and followed me. No doubt there are other circumstances and objects that terrify him whereas we would find them of no importance.

Because an autistic child believes that the world is full of frightening events and people, he refuses to look at anything directly. It has been suggested by some psychologists that these children are at the mercy of a primitive and elemental force that has not been modified by experience.

Lucien

Lucien provided me with an example of this characteristic: when he was five, we were about to set off for an excursion in the woods, and he grabbed one of the toy sponge lances that the children use for their pretend tournaments on horseback. In his confused language he mumbled, "Dinosaurs." Even though it was not easy for him to ride and hold it at the same time, I let him keep the lance because I understood that he had a deep psychological need of it.

Just as when my baby riders say they are frightened of wolves, I spoke to him in a calm, encouraging voice, telling him that we are not going to see any dinosaurs and that dinosaurs are frightened of ponies, anyway. If we did meet one, I told him, he would be much stronger, mounted on his pony. The dinosaurs were conquered and subsequently we had the same success with a dragon. I am convinced that our adventures in the woods together were an important element in eliminating these anxieties.

The pony gives the child a feeling of strength

My little riders are soon able to look at their surroundings without panic. On horseback, they can be persuaded to feel stronger than the supposed terror. They are conscious of the pony's strength and soon they take the step of understanding that these fears come from inside themselves and are not real. During this process they are constantly supported and reassured by me. On horseback, they feel the strength of the pony, and this becomes a greater reality than the imagined fears from the outside.

Steven

Steven has a love of nature: he always grasps my hand when I point at something for us to look at, whether the soaring trees or a little ants' nest at the base of a tree.

All activities at my riding club center around the animals. The children rub shoulders with a reassuring world that seems to connect with their needs. They can at last separate themselves from their security objects. Before they met the ponies, they gave so much weight to their primitive world that they could not take the vital step of integrating with the new experiences of everyday life. The animals provide the stepping stone.

Leon

When he first arrived, Leon would sit on a sofa and endlessly turn over his collection of objects. Then he began to take an interest in what was going on. He has good powers of observation, and soon he was leaving his objects and wandering about, only returning occasionally to check on them. After the session, he appeared distinctly calmer.

The importance of facial expressions

At four months old, most babies are meeting an adult's eyes. I am used to exchanging long looks with the babies in my program, and I have learned the importance at this stage of their development to avoid making expressions that might alarm them.

Babies also stare at objects and into the eyes of the pony, but autistic children do not make this vital leap without help. I sometimes use a mirror as an intermediary stage: once they have learned to accept the sight of themselves on horseback, they can begin looking at objects and other people more easily.

It is often a long process and you cannot rush this stage. If you do, you risk creating panic attacks in which the information "from outside" becomes jumbled. The child finds suddenly that he cannot relate the information either to himself or to other sources. They become merely alarm signals, and his only way of coping is to shut down the hatches or have a hysterical outburst.

If I am worried about moving too fast, I accompany my little charges, walking alongside the pony and, from time to time, exchanging glances. This will often lead to bursts of laughter, and occasionally I use mimicry to encourage the jollity, as well as pretending to hide my facial expressions. The child soon gets the idea and copies me. This little game has an important lesson to teach, that of permanence. People and objects still exist even when they are hidden from view. If they are stationary they will reappear in the same position; if moving, with reasonable provisos, they will be in the position they would have held if eyes had remained open.

Once again I must emphasize that things must not be rushed. The environment and the activities must essentially remain stable without too many changes too quickly; you must not disturb the child's habits abruptly. For several months the child must be left with the same familiar boundaries and then, you can slowly extend them. He has to be kept in the realms of the "possible," otherwise you risk seeing them retreat and furious outbursts will probably result.

Just as autistic children notice details that we hardly think important, so things we feel relevant wash over them without remark. For this reason each step we take must be logical and absolutely clear, and when repeated, in the same clear, logical way. This idea of clarity and consequence needs to be instilled in them: they need what we would call "good sense," but not in a Pavlovian way of conditioned response. We have to help them live in the real world.

Lucien

Lucien was at first fascinated by plastic objects, and I have a whole basket of these for the babies to play with. Lucien fished them out and turned them around in his hands until I decided to remove the basket in order to capture his attention. It was no good: he was furious and even refused to get on the pony, so I put the basket back in its usual place and my little rider returned.

I realized that this basket represented some primitive need that reassured the child so I would have to separate Lucien from these desired objects before we could make progress—and this is exactly what subsequently happened. He no longer needs the basket.

Lucas

When Lucas arrived for the first time he paid no attention to me at all but dived into the tack room, where he went about touching and sniffing the walls, the saddles, and harness.

It is a common enough characteristic among people with autism—both children and adults—that sight has to be associated with touch and even smell.

SMELL

Of all the senses the means by which we smell is closest to the brain. A curious characteristic of this sense is that it goes straight into long-term memory, and it is thought that this is to do with being a primitive form of communication. My pony club is not only a haven of different smells but autistic people rely on this sense more intensely than other people. As we have seen, they often smell objects and indeed people and places, in the process of recognition. It is well known that when people are anxious they give off a special odor. This odor might not be picked up by most of us but is more likely to be by an autistic person; it may transmit a feeling of fear, thereby reinforcing his wish to retreat or shut himself in. It is the same with animals who often rely on smell to differentiate between other animals.

Smell is not the best researched or understood sense. Only fairly recently was it discovered that babies a few days old can distinguish between the smell given off by material belonging to their mother's clothes and those of another woman. It is even thought that a fetus is aware of smells after six months' gestation. Premature babies born at this point have olfactory systems sufficiently developed to recognize the smell of mint and, in the case of full-term newborn babies, different smells can affect the breathing and heart rhythm. Most mothers will find that their baby is calmed by their smell, and this can be an aid to getting the child to go to sleep. I have observed that some autistic adults need to smell their horses before mounting.

Luigi

When I first held a small fir branch to Luigi's nose he pushed it away, but then he put his face so close to mine that our noses touched. I repeated this action a few times, and the next time Luigi and I met, he was holding a small fir branch. He had also acquired a small grooming brush that he obviously enjoyed sniffing, and at the end of the session he took it home.

The pony's smell, transmitted by means of the brush, forms an important link between the rider, the horse, and the pony club's surroundings. It need hardly be said that the club is a paradise of smells: hay, straw, the feed, the horses themselves, their droppings and their urine, the leather of the saddles and other tack, the saddle soap, and hoof oil for treating horses' feet. We have seen that autistic people are more conscious of smells than other people, so we can appreciate what an important role the smells play in giving them a sense of security and familiarity, and establishing markers. They are for me as well: the other day my apprentice chose to wash down one of the ponies with an apple-scented soap. I was appalled by this because it did not agree with my idea of how this pony should smell! Nature provides a battery of smells and I try to make use of this in my work.

Steven

During my rambles through the woods with Steven, we routinely passed under a pine tree that hung over the path. One day I picked a small branch from the pine, raised it to my nose, inhaled and gave it to him. He copied my action: it was as though he had newly discovered what he could achieve with his sense of smell. For the rest of the day he kept hold of the little branch and from time to time gave it back to me to smell. I noticed that he frequently had an appreciative sniff himself, and from that moment he has found pleasure in discovering lots of different smells that he can distinguish. His family has joined in the fun by pointing out lots of new smells and scents in the garden and around the house. This has opened a new sensory world for Steven; now on our walks he points excitedly toward a tree whose scent he knows.

This incident has a interesting parallel in the advice given by Françoise Dolto, "If you want to bring life to a baby who appears even to ignore a smile, wave a large leaf or that of any simple household plant, in front of his eyes, and you will see his features transformed with a smile and his lungs expanding with deep breaths. There will be a reaction, an exchange, that you may not have witnessed until now."

I encourage my autistic children to expand their repertoire of smells with those of plants, the ponies, and their surroundings. I use the sense of smell to create markers in order to give them a feeling of security and to become more aware of the differences that exist in the world. They also learn that the smell of the pine tree is "up there." And the smell of the grooming brush is waiting for him "over there" when he returns to the club; it is also the instrument with which he takes care of another living being.

It is recognized that a human being's smell presents a threat to an autistic person. An autistic child creates a protective shell that he can be said to share with the pony, that is also very sensitive to smells. One could even suppose the smell of horses and all the contents of the pony club help to conceal human smells: they create an olfactory environment that gives a feeling of security.

TASTE

Taste is not the sense that is directly engaged in the healing process; it could be considered the sense that is least thought about. Nevertheless, it can be seen to have a role. Autistic children often experience difficulty in eating certain foods and tend to stick to quite a narrow selection. However, by watching the pony eat I have found that they become more willing to expand the choice of foods they are willing to try.

Taste is closely allied to smell. After each excursion we stop near my vegetable garden and when the season permits, the children feed the ponies carrots while at the same time having a nibble themselves. In summer I encourage them to eat the strawberries and raspberries, which they adore. I am in the process of expanding my garden so that the children can increase the number of tastes they can experience.

TOUCH

"Tactile stimulation and tender caresses can help to encourage normal development in an autistic child. Children can be taught little by little to accept the comforting effect of touch. All children need this and especially autistic children," says Temple Grandin. She considered man's relationship with the horse to be a privilege.

Touch is our most primitive sense and exists over the entire surface of the body. It can detect heat and cold, shape and texture. It is the principal vehicle of the sensations we receive and of our contact with others.

The pony enables the child to learn to accept touching

A newborn foal seeks security and learns to communicate by touching its mother. The foal adores caresses and is therefore the perfect instrument for teaching the autistic child to accept the pleasures of touch. However, this does not happen right away. The softness and warmth of the pony's flesh feels foreign and uncomfortable to the touch. The best solution to kick-starting the physical bond between the child and the pony is to lift the child into the saddle and to set off at a walk. Once in the saddle the child's seat is "anchored" to the pony but through the thickness of the saddle, which allows it to be tolerated.

As I have already mentioned, I use Western saddles on my ponies and horses to provide extra support and security. Both my baby riders and autistic students seem to find a hard surface more agreeable because it establishes the limits of their body, at least in one direction. This contact is increased both by the horse's and the rider's movement. It is a transitional state to accepting the softness of direct contact with the pony.

The importance of hands

Françoise Dolto often emphasizes the importance of hands: they are the means of contact; they manipulate objects; they introduce the concept of communication through the help of objects; they develop the use of gestures and control over the immediate environment. The number of markers defining a child's field of action increases, especially when these are accompanied by words describing their action.

Babies' hands start by grasping whatever is close enough in order to put it into their mouth (hoping, perhaps, that everything in life is edible). Soon hands become the means of gathering objects, throwing them away, gathering them again. In fact, they take over as the main means of controlling the childrens' environment.

When the autistic child first begins to use his hands to explore, he uses only the tips of his fingers: his gestures are minimal, lacking in amplitude, and merely brush the surface of an object. Often they are stereotypical, repeated gestures with no apparent control.

Arriving at the point of caressing the pony marks an important stage in a child's progress. He has dared to experience something that is soft, warm, and alive. As I've mentioned, autistic children seem to have a penchant for hard plastic objects, particularly plastic play balls. On the one hand these objects are what they use for their repetitive stereotypical actions, and on the other, they help to define the limits of their body. It could be said that the repetitive actions are constantly repeating this definition and therefore bring some sense of security.

In his book *L'Énigme des Enfants Autistes* (The enigma of autistic children), Denys Ribas gives us the example of Lili to illustrate this preoccupation with hard surfaces, "When Lili takes part in a riding session she has no hesitation in entering the pony's stall and saddling it," he writes. "She is fascinated by the ponies and explores their body with her hands. She rather worries my colleagues by her fixation on the pony's hooves, its gums and teeth, all of which she feels repeatedly with the tips of her fingers."

When I have a new child at my club I observe him very carefully to see which objects or tactile sensations bring comfort: some children may respond more to hard objects, some to firm pressure. When I have established this I seek to enlarge the field and introduce soft pressure. I might stroke the palm of their hands or place their hand on the pony's soft coat while they are moving along, because the motion in itself has a calming effect. This stage is a kind of desensitizing that leads to rubbing and grooming. We know that repetitive action brings comfort, and the pony's regular movement provides this par excellence.

One day a seven-year-old was screaming and flailing about until we put him in the saddle. The wild behavior stopped abruptly, and when we started trotting, he gave me a long concentrated look. It might be worth saying at this juncture that the look of an autistic child when he accepts eye-to-eye contact is almost unnerving: it can be so penetrating as to completely unsettle you.

It is of course not uncommon for uncontrolled behavior to begin again as soon as the pony stops. It is the gentle rhythmic repeated motion that is the most powerful doctor. At first the act of stopping seems to give the children the feeling that they have been destroyed or lost their bearings.

In my experience there has been only one autistic individual—an adult—who absolutely refused to come into any contact with a horse, contact that would have allowed him to accept awareness of the "other," the world around him. All that can be said is that we were at least able to bring the horse quite close to him when we were trying to get him into the saddle.

The incident reminded me of Donna Williams in her book *Nobody Nowhere: the Remarkable Autobiography of an Autistic Girl,* where she says, "Any physical contact produced a crushing sensation as if I were falling into a black hole with an irresistible magnetic force, in which I was losing my identity, being swallowed, eaten alive, or swept away by a huge wave."

As you have seen in this chapter, the sensation of touch helps to forge an awareness of whatever surrounds the person. It could be said to "create" the surroundings because before the process begins, the autistic child hardly acknowledges them: he refuses to accept the existence of what is around him. Contact with the horse leads to an improvement in posture, followed by the beginnings of emotional awareness. Objects become a reality that can be mastered. The children learn to pick up a broom and to use it to sweep out the pony's stall, and to push the wheelbarrow and use it for its purpose, taking away the horse droppings from the stall, for instance, or transporting bags of grain or hay bales.

Naturally, all five standard senses are vitally important, but if one of them or more is lacking, or cannot be developed, there are the sixth and even seventh senses that we are aware of, which can come to the rescue: an awareness of self and a sense of balance. Some neuroscientists consider these two senses the *anchor of identity.* The awareness of self brings together the unconscious mechanisms that keep the body balanced, thanks to the combined workings of vision and muscular activity. Autistic children can have this anchor provided the environment and their activities favor the building up of their sense of identity.

HEARING

Of all the senses, this is possibly the one that produces the most acute reactions. An autistic child is hypersensitive to particular noises, and seems to be unaware of others. Volume has nothing to do with which noise gets through to him and which does not. Of the ones he notices he has to pinpoint their position and fit them into the other markers that describe a familiar environment—just as very young children do.

Autistic children usually shy away from noises that are directly in front of them, so the riding teacher's voice should come from either side or behind, only rarely from in front. Daniel Tammet said in *Born on a Blue Day,* "I used to find it very difficult taking in noises around me, and I would regularly put my hands over my ears in order to blot them out and concentrate." All people filter the information and noises that surround them,

The sound envelope

Just as we talk about a "psychic body envelope" (see p. 12), so we also use the expression "sound envelope." We all hear sounds in complicated ways. Sometimes we filter out those we don't want to hear or concentrate on those we do. We hear some sounds combined with vibrations—who has not heard a car pass by with loud music accompanied by the throb of bass? And, we hear sounds that result from something we are doing, such as dragging our fingernails across a pane of glass, knocking something over, slamming a door, pushing a wheelbarrow across gravel, or walking on creaky floorboards.

nificance of an object. As I have pointed out, these items are usually hard, not soft or giving. Tustin goes on to say, "...the hardness gives the child the feeling that the object is helping to protect him. The child appears to be concentrating on the sensation that the object gives him." This obviates any possibility of interaction with the object, or any relationship, as for instance another child would develop with a teddy bear or toy car.

Jules

Jules placed his Action Man on a bench while he had his riding lesson and retrieved it immediately afterward. For a time he had abandoned his hard object for a soft, living, responsive being. Even though he retrieved his Action Man there is now a triangular relationship, and gradually the horse "drives out" the meaningless hard item.

Luigi

As we began a session, Luigi picked up a little stick before he mounted the pony and held it tightly in his hand. After a time I was able to persuade him to abandon the stick, but when we entered the forest, we looked at the sticks lying about on the ground. I retrieved one and handed it to him. We started a game of exchange: "For you Luigi and now for me." Then I asked him to give it to his mother who was walking along with us. Later in the session, I even got him to give a stick to one of the other riders. Six months later Luigi no longer needed sticks.

When a child abandons an autistic object I offer him other things. Wandering through the woods I might pick up a strong-smelling fir branch, a prickly piece of holly, a stick, or a fir cone. Very often the child will throw it away on the first occasion, just as when I handed a cone to Luc. He threw it on the ground so I kept one and handed it to his parents. During the next session, I handed him another cone and he agreed to hold it.

Accepting a new object takes time. The child needs time to become familiar with it, and during this process, it is important to observe him closely and try to work out the stages by which he moves from refusal to acceptance. There comes a point when objects can be touched and used to produce different sensations. Out of this emerges the possibility of playing games, which is not easy for autistic children; I use my experience with the babies that ride with me to start this ball rolling.

SPACE

Autistic people have their own interpretation of space that is barely more than the area taken up by their body. As they grow in confidence so the space reaches ever further from them, but any feeling of insecurity cuts it right back.

Autistic children very often walk in a particular or peculiar way. It may appear to be hesitant, and it is not uncommon for them to walk on tiptoe as though they are reluctant to make contact with the ground. Any interaction between the child and his environment is at first chaotic—if not absent altogether—so it is not easy to make him aware of what is around him since he is not at all interested in it. He is only interested in details; space is frozen and one-dimensional. He does not distinguish between objects and people as the following example illustrates.

Arnaud

Arnaud is an autistic child who was sent to me when he was ten years of age and has been working with me for four years. Nowadays, although I can hold his stare for some time like you can with a baby, if I meet him while holding my cup of tea, he may fix his gaze on it as if it were part of me.

The "coveted" object of an autistic child is, in its way, a stepping stone to admitting the existence of "other" objects. The next stage is to persuade the child not to fix his attention exclusively on the "autistic" object but on others as well so that he begins to grasp the interaction between objects.

This, in turn, is a further step toward accepting the presence of other people and the interaction with and between them.

Steven

Steven adored playing with balls: he rolled them endlessly in his hands. I picked one of them up, and he stared fixedly at it as I placed it in a basket. I repeated the action several times while he watched me. Then we both took a ball in one of our hands and placed them in another basket a little further away. In this way Steven learned that objects are independent of him and that space exists outside him.

Theo Peeters, a Belgian neurolinguist who specializes in autism spectrum disorders and is the author of several books says in *Autism: From Theoretical Understanding to Educational Intervention,* "The fact that we know that autistic people understand things very differently from us (they have a different cognitive process) helps us to understand their strange behavior. It is their way of coping with a life that is just too complex for them. Their lack of flexibility also helps us grasp some of their illogical fears."

An autistic child tries to achieve security by dividing his perceptions into small manageable elements rather than taking in the whole picture.

Lucien

When Lucien came back to the pony club for his second session, he went immediately to the large ring where he had ridden on the first occasion. He walked around it without taking any notice of me, even though I was walking by his side, apparently to reestablish his markers—that is, his familiar landmarks, whether visual, auditory, or olfactory—that defined the place.

I usually start autistic children in the small rectangular riding ring for this very reason: the children need to establish their markers with ease as it gives them this feeling of security—an essential precursor to making progress. I decided on modest proportions and a quadrangular shape after a great deal of research, and I am particularly indebted to Paul Sivadon and François Gantheret, authors of a book about the reeducation of mental functions, who describe this space as "a familiar one that can easily be explored and one that the child has no difficulty in visualizing and remembering."

The child soon feels at home and knows exactly where he is in relation to the familiar objects around him. Nothing changes very much there—with the exception of different ponies and the other children. The familiarity of the surroundings and the comforting sensation of being on the pony's back gives him the confidence that he needs in order to start acknowledging that there are other children in the arena and perhaps he can imitate them.

How the child perceives space

Until a baby is four months old, he perceives space in separate bits. Rather in the manner of an autistic child he makes no connection between various senses: hearing, touch, and sight. When he approaches eighteen months, he is coordinating sight and manual dexterity: he is grasping objects and beginning to arrange them to his liking in the space around him. Up until two years old, the space in which he exists is that of his own body. The Swiss psychologist and philosopher, Jean Piaget, who made an important study of the way in which a child's mind works, refers to it as "topological space."

Also before four months old, the movement of an object—for instance, something the child is grasping—and the child himself are all one. At about ten months, the child begins to make the distinction between himself and an object, and he begins to accept that things keep their shape. This stage is allied to the coordination of movement and is a particularly crucial one for autistic children.

Jean-Claude Barrey, an authority on ethology, has some pertinent observations about the spatial perceptions of animals. "As with young children," he writes, "the spatial awareness of animals is topological, that is to say, it embraces the most elementary elements: proximity, separation, continuity, and the degree to which it surrounds them."

Every child, whether in difficulty or not, appreciates the beauty of the horses and ponies that live so happily in this wonderful place in the middle of the forest of Reno-Valdieu. Peace reigns here and a sense of complete security. The setup of the enclosed spaces that make up my facility is carefully conceived and structured.

When children first arrive I let them wander about taking it all in, and then I accompany them, pointing out each area. The first space they see is the paddock by the entrance, then there is the tack room, and then the small riding ring with its toys and play objects. I allow my manner and the words I use to be guided by the information that the child sends me. I soon become aware of how much he is capable of absorbing. If he is frightened of speech, I keep quiet.

The very young ones tend to explore only part of the riding arena: the area where the toys are kept and where they play. The objects, for the most part, are made of hard plastic but there are also balloons and balls of various sizes. These objects will constitute their markers, things that will define the space for them. When they are overcome by proceedings they can retreat to this area and play with and handle the objects.

The child gets the measure of a space by first getting the measure of his own body. This is achieved through contact with the play objects, taking note of their position—and again when they are moved—and finally, by their moving their own body around the space.

Ernest

There are baskets around the perimeter of the play arena filled with objects of different shapes: both cubes and balls. Up until this moment Ernest had been obsessed with sticks that he found in the woods, but now he took a fancy to cubes. He picked up one of them and handed it to me, and then in a completely calm and considered way threw it on the ground as though trying to demonstrate something to me. I watched him closely as he extended his arm in the direction of the cube pointing directly at it. We both looked at it intently and I said, repeating myself a number of times, "On the ground." I always try to use very few and simple phrases with the autistic children because of the difficulty they experience in understanding several concepts at the same time.

Ernest watched me closely and then showed me, pointing with his finger, the rafters along the roof. We studied them together and I said a number of times, "Up high." By moving his arms about, Ernest had discovered the space he inhabits. Once he understood, he made another move: he tried to hand a cube to a little girl of his own age, three-and-a-half. At first, he was too far away so he moved his body toward her until he was able to hand over the cube.

I remember Catherine Mathelin-Vanier saying that it was as if Ernest was discovering his own bodily limits at the same time as those of the building he was in, and this was achieved by moving his arms around. The movement was an essential part of the process. His connection with his surroundings also depended on his sense of touch when he felt the cube, as well as the varying sensations he received by using his muscles and tendons that allowed him to flex his arms and point them in the direction of his choice. They gave him a sense of where he was in the space of the arena, and this had implications to do with seeing. By pointing at the cube on the ground, he was developing a sense of depth and at the roof rafters a sense of height. The simple act of throwing a cube onto the ground had led the way to all these steps in comprehension. The arena's walls that surrounded him, the ceiling with its wooden beams, the ground onto which he flung the cube, the fact that he and the ponies were moving about in the space, all helped him to make the mental leap of understanding something about his surroundings and situation.

When handing the cube to another child, Ernest became aware of his position in space by moving the object toward its goal, then moving his own body. He also became aware of the feel and shape of the object: to him the cube with its hard corners and angles was a new shape. He had entered the third dimension. He had discovered something about his body; experienced movement through space; taken in that space was not flat; and realized that there was someone else whom he could approach through the space. It was only through movement that this step was achieved.

Steven

I tried to attract Steven's attention by pointing to a dead birch tree that had mushrooms growing on the trunk. When I said, "Mushrooms," Steven immediately pointed to the ground, which was logical since in his experience that is where they grew. But then I pointed to the dead tree again and he saw them in this unaccustomed place and pointed at other trees saying, "Mushrooms."

In this way Steven learned that things are not always fixed immovably in space. The understanding of space around one depends primarily on our visual faculty. Visual markers give a feeling for how far away an object is, how low down or how high up.

Both Ernest and Steven at first had difficulty grasping the concept of space; they were too fixed on details and had a problem with putting them together and working out their relationship, one with another.

The concept of space and movement within it

Thanks to the riding and play areas I have devised, I am able to develop the riders' visual acuity: they begin to piece together the parameters of space, the fact that things can be near or far, behind or in front, high or low. In the smaller of the two spaces, they begin to be interested in the position of the various objects. This leads to a desire to explore for themselves and all the time, they feel completely secure: the landmarks are there in familiar positions; everything is under control. Exploration can proceed without anxiety.

The pony is a big help in instilling this idea of space since it is the "vehicle" moving the person from one position to another; it carries the child, who is carrying the ball or cube from one basket to another and when the first basket is full and the second empty, the concept of filling and emptying, as well as containing and being contained, is also touched on. Since the pony moves about, the child is freed from the necessity of having to decide to move himself—the pony does it for him. The child can concentrate on exploration.

Learning about "Yes!" and "No!"

When Steven made as if to disappear from sight as we were about to start a session, he would look at me to see if I was going to stop him and say "No!" Now that he has learned the meaning of "yes" and "no," he needs situations that will test these meanings to ensure they are correct. Most children pick this up very quickly but a child with autism can take a long time: all the discoveries have to be tested and verified, and he has to be reassured and supported.

So, when Steven deliberately knocks over an object in the arena, he is waiting to see if he is told not to do that. "The posts holding up the jump bar as well as the cones must be left where I put them, Steven," I might say. I am helping him to differentiate between what is allowed and what is not, and this also helps to define space: he can go here but not there. It structures the thoughts but it cannot be rushed: the "no" has to be accepted internally before it affects his external behavior. "No" has to be sensitively handled and repeated calmly many times so that he gets used to it. Autistic children are so fragile—it's like they are skating on the edge of the ice, ready at any moment to fall into the water and disappear.

An autistic child has to have his field of interest enlarged, he has to be helped to break out of his segmented world of desired objects that absorb his attention and his energy, and he needs to learn to accept that every situation is in some way complex. I begin by observing closely what markers an autistic child has chosen to limit his attention, and then I use that knowledge to widen his field of comprehension.

Arnaud

Arnaud was obsessed with the balls to begin with, so I introduced a cube that I handed to him as he sat on his pony. He threw it onto the ground, but I noticed that he followed the trajectory. I picked it up and gave it back to him. He accepted it from me and threw it down again, but this time he glanced at my face as he threw it. We repeated this little game several times not only because it was a form of interaction with Arnaud but because it gave him a sense of depth. From where he was seated in the saddle, the distance to the ground was enough to make him aware of it. It was not long before he abandoned the object. We commonly talk about autistic children being in a one-, or at most, two-dimensional world. In this little experiment Arnaud was toying with a third dimension: depth and distance.

Luigi

Luigi was a small child lacking any self-confidence. I put him on a large pony so that his eyes were above the level of adults on foot. This produced an increase in confidence to the extent that he called his parents to point out events around him like the approach of Cocase, the stable dog.

Two- and three-dimensional space

Donald Meltzer in his book *Explorations in Autism: A Psychoanalytic Study* describes this problem: "The way an autistic person behaves points to his preference for one-, or at most, two-dimensional space. In one dimension, the child is often rigid, immobile, or engages in a repetitive action such as revolving endlessly around a floor lamp. In a two-dimensional example he could be obsessed with a sound at the same time as revolving round the lamp."

Contact with the pony provides the intermediary by which the child slowly accepts outside stimulation and allows him to escape from one- or two-dimensional space. I usually begin by working on eye/hand contact, suggesting little exercises such as taking a ball from one basket to another that is some distance away. By bringing into play sensory stimulation, the sight of objects that are then handled, and by getting the child to imitate actions, the pleasure of actually doing things for oneself is awoken. This brings emotion to the equation, and understanding follows.

Learning about the complexity of space and the objects that fill it

The pony is the vehicle that allows the child to conquer the space about him: he learns to reach up for a ball, to look up to the treetops, to move sideways, forward, and backward in order to fetch objects. Part of this takes place outside the arena, in the surrounding woods where we can use steep inclines for going up and down. Looking behind as he ascends and descends, and then straight ahead when he reaches the level ground, helps him to rotate his trunk. His eyes are no longer fixed on a single object; he becomes flexible and mobile as his body axis assumes its proper position.

A baby already has innate abilities when he is born: he learns rapidly and at two or three months he is exchanging looks with others, but an autistic child is blocked until, with the help of the pony and the teacher, he can see the way ahead, though any instruction often has to be mimed and frequently repeated before it is understood and leads to learning about interaction with others.

But the happy fact is that an autistic child is capable, with the right help, of learning to understand the concept of space, and that objects can be moved and removed without the world coming to an end. Once his eyes can be taught to follow an object while it is moving, he begins to develop hand/eye coordination.

I always use the smaller of my two arenas to start with: the child can take in the whole area with his eyes, can easily establish his markers and become aware of the position of each object in relation to himself and other objects. As I have mentioned, my students are usually fascinated by the colored balloons that are in various places and at different heights off the ground.

When a child fixes his eyes on a particular balloon or ball, I sometimes rotate it so that he can grasp the association between the hand, the movement, and seeing the movement take place. Often, having watched me do this he will want to touch the ball with his own hands. The pony takes him toward it, and he finds himself touching it from a different higher angle than I do because I am on foot. I may approach the ball from the right or the left side or straight ahead and if he wants to take the ball in his hands and throw it, he has to lean forward or twist his torso this way or that. If he follows the ball with his eyes as he throws it he begins to understand the depth of the space. Sometimes the ball falls behind a rider or an object and then reappears as the person or as he moves a little. This gives the child the idea of the permanence of the object: it can disappear but doesn't stop existing.

We all form an idea of the world about us from whatever our senses register. Communication usually requires gestures, sight, sound or touch but can also rely on something less tangible. Let me give you an example of what I mean.

Steven

It was winter; nightfall came before the session was over. Steven's mother had told me that Steven was frightened of the dark, so I took his hand as we set off for a walk in the woods and said, "Come with me, Steven. I'm not afraid of the dark." He showed no fear on our short walk. His mother told me that from that day he was no longer afraid. It must have been at least in part as a result of my own confident, calm demeanor as we set out together.

The transmission of ideas by subtle changes in our tone of voice, the direction of our eyes, and our nonverbal communication are of prime importance to autistic people. They can be more sensitive than normal people and are all too easily thrown by anything negative, so it is essential to be calm, not raise your voice, think positive and loving thoughts, and be aware of your facial expressions.

TIME

An autistic child appears to live outside the idea of time: the future does not exist for him. He lives a circular existence filled with constantly repeated actions not unlike very small children banging a toy repeatedly on the ground. He lives outside conventional linear time where there is a past, a present, and a future; his stereotypical behavior is an expression of stationary time.

This is automatically invaded by the rhythmic movement of the pony that substitutes for a structured world marked by the passage of time. If I help the child do a rising trot I accompany it with the words, "tic tac"— "tic" is for the upward motion and "tac" for the down. The one follows the other automatically: the child simply cannot remain in one "blink" of time. I have noticed that in the mind of an autistic child the concept of time is defined by his environment and in particular the parts he has mastered: the objects and spaces he has become familiar with through his activities and the people with whom he has had contact.

Lucien and Jules

Lucien has been working at my pony club for four years. He now speaks lucidly and can think ahead—an important advance. He explained that he was going to his grandparents for his vacation, and he knew the dates.

Similarly, Jules knows that he comes for riding therapy on a Friday. He has accepted the day as one of his landmarks and he is thinking ahead.

Learning about time past, time present, and time future

For another child the marker could be the journey here or to some activity he engages in after our session. Whatever it is, it requires frequent repetition, and acceptance without anxiety.

As Michel Lemay, author and professor of psychiatry in Montreal says, it is from this mix that the child constructs his concept of time: time past, time present, and time future. The constant interplay of time passing, his surroundings, the people he knows, and testing himself against the environment and the people—all these things help to build a road for himself, one that acknowledges the present but remembers the past and accepts that events that have not yet taken place will come about. This new state is in marked contrast to the one he was stuck in: one that appeared to exist outside the concept of time in which the past was confused with the present and the future did not exist.

Jules

Each week I am sent three groups of children from a center that specializes in "problem children." Six-year-old Jules was one child who adapted without difficulty to the pony club. I always greeted him and said goodbye, as I do to all the children, with a light kiss on the cheek. To the astonishment of his caregivers, he accepted this bodily contact without protest; they said that he never allowed any physical contact. What the caregivers did not know was that Jules had been with me before—when he was three. Though he was still not at the stage where he could remember the past in the normal sense, the agreeable feelings he had as a three-year-old were still with him. If he had had a bad experience then, that would have stayed with him, too.

Learning good habits, including delayed gratification

Greeting someone on arrival and saying goodbye is all part of learning to structure time and space, and instilling habits is a precursor to having any concept of the future.

Autistic children have to learn to plan for the future. When they start with me, we concern ourselves with the present alone, but when they start to make plans we talk about all the events that punctuate their lives in a regular way. "Working on the computer is at 4:00 pm!"

The concept of time is full of rhythmical events such as mealtimes, night, and day, so there is a lot to build on. I structure the sessions so that certain games take place at regular times and in a familiar sequence. The idea of waiting—that is, delayed gratification—has to be introduced: I make them wait for a few moments before mounting or grabbing one of the balls or cubes in the ring. However, I only start working on this idea when I feel the children are ready to accept a little frustration. When they begin with me there is no delay—everything is ready.

LANGUAGE

Language is the last piece of the puzzle to be put into place. The child soon becomes aware of the messages that pass between him and the pony— whether they will stop, turn, trot, or canter, and how to cope with uneven ground. When I see this, I put words to each change in pace or situation. At first, my words will be copied in the form of mimicry; gradually they assume their intended meaning.

Luigi

Luigi lets me know, without saying anything, that he has seen the steep descent ahead of us, so I might say, "Going down, Luigi."

chapter 7

Discovering the Body

"When autistic people put their trust in another person they sometimes feel so close that they cannot distinguish between the other person and themselves. This was the case with Valentine, and one day I had to say to her that my body was not part of her body, and therefore it was not possible for me to deal with all her anguish unless she recognized that I was a different person. Only then could I help her. 'No, Valentine, I simply cannot step into your shoes and be you.' She recoiled as if in horror, and I wondered for a moment if she was about to go to pieces. Then I told her I understood how very difficult it was, and she calmed down. For the first time we didn't have a hysterical scene. She began to cry, but the tears were real and as they coursed down her cheeks, she said, 'The house is crumbling.'"

—Catherine Mathelin-Vanier

Ernest showed me the different parts of his body to which he had given the names, "Dad," "Mom," or "What's that?" As he moved his arms to point or touch I realized he was also learning about space. I discussed this with Catherine Mathelin-Vanier who commented that this was an interesting development. Before he started riding, Ernest only referred to the different parts of his body as "Dad" or "Mom." The fact that he had added, "What's that?" indicated he no longer thought that his body was part of theirs.

Touch leads to understanding

An autistic child seems to put the different parts of his body together by building it up from another person's body. As he discovers his own body he finds the need to touch these limbs, and at that point, I name them with him. I have observed that, as a rule, an autistic child learns by experience that often has to be patiently repeated, but this must not be confused by the repetitive mannerisms that can occupy their entire attention. These are not part of the learning process.

The pony, through its constant stable movement, sends signals that help the child to distinguish between the outside and inside of his body and gradually to identify of all the different parts of his body. I try to sense this awareness so that we can name the body parts together. Little by little the child constructs his own body until it is a whole person.

Steven

Steven touches his nose, we name it, and then he touches mine, followed by our mouth, eyes, arms, and hands. He feels these different limbs and body parts both on me and on himself, and at the same time he sees them and hears the name. By touching these limbs one after another, Steven brought into play several of his senses and began to understand how they interact with each other. Like all autistic children, he can be hypersensitive to some forms of stimulation and insensitive to others, but he is beginning to accept outside influences and integrate them into his understanding.

Today Steven was testing his balance: he leaned to the right and then to the left until he almost fell off the pony, but he recovered in time. He was carrying out these experiments with three other children, and when the session was over they all had a good canter, something Steven can do superbly. When he came to a stop I walked up to him, and he put his hand out, stroked my face, touching my nose and my eyes like a baby discovering his mother.

Discovering different parts of the body

The pony is in contact with various parts of the child's body in an uninterrupted and noninvasive way. The child cannot escape and accepts the contact that plunges him into a veritable bath of different sensations. He becomes aware of his limbs, he can smell the pony, he can see and feel it moving, and he can hear the sounds of the hooves and the pony breathing. These sensations help him to understand the difference between sensations that strike him from outside and his own interior feelings. It is a constant filling out of his world map.

Soon this includes accepting that the teacher is not part of the horse. The need to touch parts of the teacher's body is part of the child's learning process, accepting that his body is separate from that of his teacher and the pony, that they each have their own individual character.

There is a similarity in the relationship that develops between a "baby rider" and his pony. Babies are often remarkably adept riders, in that from a very early age they adopt a good riding position with their head up and balanced, only requiring another's hand held low down along their back near the saddle as support. They think of themselves as part of the pony, like a centaur. They only discover their own body bit by bit: first, that they need to use their hands to stop the pony without changing their body position; then, that they need to use their feet to get the pony moving.

When a baby holds an object he sees it as an extension of his hand, and he speaks about it as though it were his hand. If he has not been able to get hold of an item he might say, "No hands." When his feet slip out of the stirrups (with very small children their feet are tucked into the stirrup leathers) he may say, "No more feet," or "Feet broken." Just as in the case of the baby, the pony enables the autistic child to put himself together—though the journey is longer and much more precarious.

The pony leads the way out of "prison"

Steven

When we first became acquainted, Stephanie, Steven's mother, told me that Steven would sometimes batter his head against the wall. This is not an uncommon habit of autistic children and is part of their discov-

ery of bodily limits. When she told me this I suggested two sessions a week at my pony club so that Steven could build up the awareness of his body. After only four sessions he stopped banging his head and became more manageable and calm.

In fact, Steven's progress, like that of Ernest and Lucien, was quite spectacular, and I am of the opinion that only a pony can produce this speed of change in which the child allows himself to grow and be more flexible, both physically and emotionally.

A baby soon learns to love, feel, explore, imitate, and look for things. An autistic child needs the help of a guide to take these essential steps out of his self-imposed "prison." He simply cannot do it alone; he has enough trouble just surviving. Fortunately, the pony is the perfect intermediary to carry him safely into the real world. He pieces the concept of his body together, even though it does not form a whole at first, because the movement of the pony and contact with it awakens parts of his mind that have been inaccessible and asleep since an early stage of his life. It teaches him to communicate with another living being and soon leads to his discovery of the different concepts of an "outside" and an "inside." It reintroduces elasticity into his approach to everything, something that has been missing since the child retreated into his closed world.

This is such an overwhelming process that in the early stages, I deliberately limit the variety of sensations. You do not want the child to take in too much in a short space of time—if he is exposed to too many new stimuli, he may panic and close up again, or return to his "autistic objects." Contact with the pony is not unlike contact with the mother that was so cruelly interrupted at an early moment. It teaches the child once again to accept bodily contact with another living creature.

By "holding" the child safely the pony helps him combat mortal terror

According to Frances Tustin, the crisis in an autistic child's life is triggered by the separation from the mother at birth: it was too sudden and too violent. Most authors agree that autistic children are, on the whole, very intelligent and sensitive. Unfortunately, they become aware far earlier than they should that they cannot understand what is taking place. Françoise Dolto writes, "The trouble with autistic people is that they are more intelligent than us!" They become aware of the separation from their mother before they can deal with it, and this causes them to disintegrate, trying to make up for their loss by getting rid of the self—a sort of terrible, self-destructive action—in order not to relive the loss of the mother. Again Frances Tustin says that in order to escape from a mortal terror, the child builds himself a protective cover, like a seashell that goes on producing more and more layers until it cannot move or function.

The pony is the best protection against this terror; it is not in any way a threat but a calming, reassuring, and protective presence.

How does the pony do it?

D.W. Winnicot writes in his book *Maturational Processes and the Facilitating Environment: Studies in the Theory of Emotional Development* that you have to think of a baby as an immature being that is constantly on the edge of such an extreme state of anxiety that we cannot really picture it. However, the child's anxiety consists of just a few variations:
1. The fear of disintegrating into little pieces.
2. The fear of continuously falling.
3. The fear of having no connection to his body.
4. The feeling of helplessness brought on by the body not being aligned so that it can function properly.

How does the pony help these conditions?
1. It gathers the disparate pieces together.
2. It holds the child safely and stops the falling sensation.
3. It puts the child in touch with his body.
4. It sorts out his alignment and posture.
5. And, of course, it exercises a continuous calming effect through its gentle rocking movement.

It is astonishing how the children's spines become straighter within a short time, and as we have seen, this allows all sorts of movements that were not possible before they straightened out, as well as enabling them to look at an object or person without difficulty. The significance of good posture is often not understood: if someone is hunched forward, the vital organs are cramped and almost certainly cannot function correctly. Blood flow from the heart to the brain may be impaired and mobility is certainly reduced.

My little riders often seem to be on the point of exploding when they feel they cannot grasp some outside event. It is hideously difficult to understand what is going on in the mind of autistic children so I concentrate like mad to pick up any signals they send in order to comfort them with the help of the ponies. Sensation arriving from outside is so often seen as intrusive.

Mothers can assuage this anxiety with most babies by responding to their cries, and it may be that a caress is all that is needed or simply a feeding. With an autistic child this does not work because he has not allowed the bond with his mother to form. Moreover, his skin feels like it is on fire when he is touched, and all sensations arriving from outside seem too strong to endure, so his only option is to retreat into his protective shell. He substitutes repetitive and stereotypical actions.

It is the gift of the pony that it can mediate between the child and the outside world, enabling him to reestablish contact. The autistic child, rocked by the pony's comforting rhythm, can return to the secure feeling he had in his mother's womb and start again at a pace introduced by the pony that will not cause him to panic and close up. At last, he finds himself in an environment he can cope with: he can piece himself together as the real progress begins, and he dares to abandon his very early point of development where he had become so tragically stuck.

Putting their body together

I have noticed that "baby riders" also discover their body bit by bit. The pony, thanks to all the different physical sensations it provides, is a great help in speeding up the process and piecing it together. As a general rule riding enables a person to discover his body in this piecemeal way because almost every part of the body is brought into play by its motions.

When "aids" are applied—hands, legs, feet, seat, body weight, and eyes—they all help to establish a dialogue with the horse for it is not a "one-way operation." As the rider becomes more experienced, he learns to "listen" to the horse and respond to what he hears. What is more, the dialogue never ceases, and therefore the learning process continues for as long as a person rides.

I also think that even before a child begins to interact with the horse, there is an automatic "improving" effect produced by the movement on the rider's seat, and therefore, on his posture.

Children respond more quickly than adults and it is difficult to imagine someone continuing to ride like a sack of potatoes. It seems to be an automatic result that the child begins to feel the unity of his body: it no longer feels like unconnected jigsaw pieces. When the children first experience the sensation of their body in movement, as soon as they have dismounted, they will often stand in front of a mirror, touching different parts of each other's body as part of the journey to discover their own.

The pony enables the children to have a "physical conversation"; they have no choice. It is impossible for the rider to cut himself off from receiving physical sensations—and also from responding. In a sense it is an education that cannot be avoided: the position of the rider's body, his body tone, coordination, ability to grasp something, all improve. What is more, the child is suddenly in a raised position where he looks down on what is happening around him and at people on foot. This raised position probably gives him confidence that he has never felt until this moment. If he can dominate the pony maybe he can dominate the world!

A whole gamut of new thoughts begins to result from his improved body position, tone, and coordination. Because an autistic child has no concept of his own psychic body envelope, he has little awareness of the envelope of space, but the body has to construct itself in space. It is noticeable that during this part of the process, children often run off very fast and in every direction. It is the same with very little children: they have no concept of danger or of any limits.

A specialist in psychomotor function, Severine Joyeux, came to watch me working with Steven. She saw, at first, how he was all over the place, both physically and in the way he moved. Soon we could see the pony's effect of seeming to hold the pieces in place; he was beginning to become an entity and not a disjointed collection of limbs and thoughts.

Steven

Quite soon after I had begun working with Steven I saw him push himself off the saddle and back toward the tail until he was sitting over the pony's hocks. In a way, I thought that this was an interesting advance because he was no longer afraid of contact with the softness of the pony's coat. I quickly removed the saddle so that he was in full contact with the animal, and he put up with this new experience for a full five minutes.

During his next session, Steven began to tilt his body into extreme positions but not so he lost his balance. In fact, he demonstrated his athletic prowess by being able to survive such dangerous positions without falling off. This was a proprioceptive demonstration that showed us how much control Steven had over his limbs. I might also add the pony put up with what was happening, just as a mother would with her child.

Accepting new acquaintances

Afterward while I was watering the arena I introduced Lucien to Severine and asked him if he would like to go and get his pony ready with her. He was most insistent that he should have the pony called Figaro, and as they set off together, with me trailing a little to the rear, he began to play hide-and-seek, a game I often play with him. So here he was initiating a game and demanding a particular pony; he had moved beyond the passive stage.

Severine and Lucien went into the paddock to saddle up the pony, but then Lucien turned to me to help him into the saddle: he was falling back on his known support and acknowledging me as the person who knows how to do things. Once in the saddle Lucien was keen to show off his skills to Severine; he was at ease with himself and able to make contact with this new acquaintance. He had begun to recognize the other person, not just himself.

Steven also went through this stage of interacting with me. He suddenly jumped off the pony in midsession and then stared at me with a naughty little smile as if to see whether he had gone too far. I think it is important to understand this stage and to continue introducing challenges in order to broaden their horizons. They must not be allowed to settle into a sort of false normality at too early a stage.

chapter 8

The Birth of Language, Relationships, and Imagination

"One must never think that because these children do not speak to you, it is not worth speaking to them. Trying to say something to an autistic child implies that you are trying to listen to him and, in fact, the smallest gesture, signal, or sound is communicating something to us."
—Catherine Mathelin-Vanier

think that autistic children want to communicate but are shy of trying to because it is all too violent for them. They need the intervention of a horse to hold them, "embrace" them, and lead them toward the idea of communication with others. They are hypersensitive to other people's emotions but have no protection against them, and since communication is normally verbal, this presents the worst possible approach. The horse does not speak and makes no verbal demands, whereas a person appears to attack them with words and looks, which they hate.

Catherine Mathelin-Vanier says, according to Margaret Mahler in her book *Infantile Psychosis and Early Contributions*, that the children's aim is to protect themselves against the world. In order to achieve this, they function as if in "hallucinatory denial" of understanding. People often think these children are deaf, such is their inability to react to someone's voice. They are, in effect, persecuted by the mere presence of another person, let alone his voice and his looks, which constitute an apparent danger. This can apply to any "outside" person because he is understood to be a threat by just existing—and this is unbearable. (In fact, this is what took place in Steven's case. He was thought to be deaf by a doctor and even treated for it. As a result, he made it clear he did not want to see the doctor again.)

They themselves are not making any demands on the other person: Leo Kanner, a psychiatrist and physician known for his work related to autism, talks about the need for "sameness" in this respect. The presence of another person who poses the risk of interference and change in their petrified world, unleashes panic and terror.

Contact with the pony is the first step toward communicating

Contact with the pony is the primary means of returning to the "archaic" moment in time when the child closed down the hatches. From that moment, no relationship was possible because the child first has to construct the concept of his psychic body envelope. This cannot be achieved without accepting physical stimuli on the surface of the body, and anxiety has lead to blocking these so that communication is no longer possible. Contact with the pony allows a return to this critical moment in time so that the necessary stages can be lived through: the threshold of anxiety is lowered, the body learns to assume its proper shape and balance, sensory perceptions begin to be accepted and integrated, as is the concept of space, and finally, relationships become possible when the stages are lived through.

Jacques Lacan, a French psychoanalyst, psychiatrist, and author, talks about the impossibility of an autistic child communicating because he has no tools to make it possible. The tools of communication are all in the hands of the other person. It requires an experienced analyst to convince the child that he can and does understand a message the child is sending. However, I am able to get around this problem—thanks to the ponies. Because I am in such close contact with my ponies, I am considered to be a kind of pony. I took a course with Jean-Claude Barrey (the French dressage master and author of several books) in ethology—the study of animal behavior—and he reinforced this concept: in order to truly understand horses you have to become one of them.

Daniel Tammet, in his book about his own experience, *Born on a Blue Day: Life with High-functioning Autism and Savant Syndrome,* talks about the complete absence of relationships with other people. "I remember," he says "neither the name nor the face of a single other child during my first years at school. I lived under the impression that they were something I had to put up with and get used to and steer around, rather than individuals whom I could get to know or with whom I could play games."

Temple Grandin also mentions this lack of any meaningful relationship. "I was hardly aware of the other children; I preferred my own private little world."

An autistic child probably cuts himself off from any relationship, say the psychoanalysts, ironically, because they are too sensitive to relationships.

"The other person was never allowed to exist because a drama occurred that stopped the child from engaging with the world," says Catherine Mathelin-Vanier. And so the autistic person remains both physically and mentally in a world that is hived off from that which most other people know.

At my pony club my autistic riders take part in activities together with other children, and this develops their social skills. An autistic child needs a lot of time to observe and piece together the individual events that surround him. In contrast, a little baby will pick up the details of disparate events, and because of his determination to make sense of what is going on, he begins to piece them together at a young age.

I concentrate on what is positive and ignore the difficulties

Dealing with autistic people is fraught by setbacks because it is so difficult to put yourself in their shoes and to understand the chaos that reigns inside them. Usually physicians use their own understanding as a guide and make allowances according to the age of the subject. In my case, I pay little attention to the perceived difficulties: I push forward using all the information that the individual gives me, though I often have to work hard to extract it. There is always information, but you can be sure that it is buried, and a smile or a look will one day be the reward.

First the straightforward word; other meanings emerge later

My work with my very youngest riders has helped to show me the way and given me the determination to awaken the autistic children from their state of mind. When a baby starts to learn the meaning of words and concepts, each word will, at first, have a single meaning, each object a single function. Other meanings emerge later. A baby begins by using a word like "teddy" to describe his bear and we are probably never aware of the moment when the child understands that the word can also be used as a name.

An autistic child has to go through this same stage, and it cannot be rushed. I imagine that certain words might be terrifying for him, for instance, "I'll keep an eye on it," will no doubt be taken literally. The child might reply, "Your eye is on the pony?" I recall a three-year-old saying to me when I remarked that the sun was going to bed, "No, the sun is on the ground." I once told a four-year-old to move in the same direction as the line of ponies. Unfortunately, the expression we use in riding, "Take the head of the pony" (meaning to lead it) was understood by the child to mean that he had to take the pony's head in his hands. He was so upset by the idea that he did not want to return for another session with me. It was only when his keenly observant grandmother understood and the misunderstanding was put right, that the child returned.

That was a lesson for me, and ever since I am extremely careful in my choice of words. When a child does not understand something he usually lets you know, but not so, the autistic child. He bottles it up inside. However, I believe that understanding can begin to grow with the right conditions: notably a coherent approach in the stable and its surroundings. The communication I have with my ponies is natural, spontaneous, and intuitive; it's the same with the children and it works.

Everything is taken literally

Because autistic children have so few means of communication compared to other children, they are peculiarly sensitive to the choice of words. You have to be direct with no suggestion of lying or deception. They are incredibly sensitive and take everything you say literally: any show of emotion will be amplified. This is why I place such importance on the simple act of smiling. To adapt a famous saying, "Smile and the world will smile with you!" The French have a lovely expression: *joie de vivre*. As with so many expressions in all languages, it is sometimes difficult to find one in another language that exactly translates it without losing something. In this case, the meaning is fairly obvious: "The joy of life"—and this is what I try to get across to my autistic children.

Again I draw on my experience with my "baby riders." I notice that as young as four or five months, they are busily looking about them at all the goings-on at the pony club. They appear to enjoy the expressions on people's faces, or the sounds of the voices and the ponies. They even appear to distinguish between happy expressions and ones of surprise or displeasure. Actually, I've noticed that expressions of joy and displeasure appear to be the first ones to register with an autistic child who is making progress.

Throughout this book I have referenced the theory that when we are on horseback, we go back and in a way rejoin a primitive moment in our life. I have used my awareness of this state to transmit a feeling of security and *joie de vivre* to the children. The very serious accident that I had when I was a young woman also helped. When I first emerged from the coma, suspended between life and death, all I saw were shadows. My first contact was with a kind woman who looked after our family. She took care of me without saying anything, but her smile and the way she looked at me said everything that needed to be said: she gave me the will to live; she gave me a feeling of optimism; she smiled and I shared her joy. I have never lost this feeling and my life's work is giving something of it to the children I care for.

Jules

At the Institute of Medicine and Psychology where I work part-time, I found myself eating lunch next to Jules, a twelve-year-old. Jules had recently made good progress in his use of speech and also in the way he engaged with his surroundings. He still required a good deal of help in order to structure his conversation, so my colleague, Lucy, would often sit with him during meals in order to provide him with the support he needed.

On this occasion Jules was keen to show me the progress he had made. He told me how he had recently made a mess during a meal. Lucy had sat beside him at the following meal, and he told me that she had been cross with him. He behaved well on that occasion and he was fully aware that both Lucy and I were now pleased with him.

So here we have an example of a young boy forming connections with two other people and understanding the emotions involved in creating and solving an incident. He was able to share his emotions with me and acknowledge that I was a separate person, distinct from him. Here was real communication. This incident also touches on the fact that when an autistic person learns to do something with one person, he does not automatically understand that he has to do it with another. It was something of an achievement when, as with Jules, this happened.

Anxiety inhibits relationships

I have already touched on the problems of newly born babies but would like to explore the subject some more. I've said that a weightless baby in the womb finds the shock of being separated from his mother almost too much to bear. There is a theory that at this very early point in a baby's development, his first view of his mother's face could be interpreted as seeing the "enemy." It is only when the baby begins to return his mother's smile, usually at about three months old, but sometimes sooner, that he totally overcomes this primitive reaction. Before this moment takes place the baby makes his wishes known by crying and making agitated movements with his arms and legs. An autistic baby, however, will not be able to climb out of early primitive state of development: he may continue to avoid eye contact.

At about eight months, another period of anxiety makes itself felt. Usually, a baby will by now recognize his mother, even if he does not smile, but will be alarmed when there is another face other than hers looking at him. Three mothers of autistic children that I know were so worried by these signs that they consulted a doctor thinking that there were problems with their child's hearing or vision.

In my pony club this problem is bypassed because children of that age find it easy to look at the pony. They allow themselves to be supported by my arm, and the rocking effect of the pony's walk has an immediate calming effect. While the pony is moving they will even look at my face, but the moment it stops they need to be with their mother again. And, because of the ponies I very rarely see examples of "eight-month anxiety."

However, strangely there is sometimes an even more problematical period between the age of eighteen months and two years when some children, in particular boys, are highly distressed at being separated from their mother and may not even be calmed by setting off on the pony. Recently, I was working with an eight-year-old who developed severe anorexia at eighteen months, when his mother returned to work. He stopped eating and ended up in hospital; he still has severe problems.

At eighteen months babies usually develop their sense of identity and become aware of other people's existence. It is the age when they recognize themselves in a mirror. It is also the age when they take most readily to riding and appreciate the new relationship with a pony; it goes well with their need to affirm their own personality. With autistic children everything happens more slowly. I remember a sixteen-month-old rider who took a whole year before engaging with his environment and getting his bodily axis correct. Another child needed four months of patient work before he allowed himself to engage with me.

Steven

Steven was a typical autistic child: after he was born he cried whenever he was separated from his mother. At eight months, he refused to leave his stroller. At two years old, he withdrew completely from the world. The family consulted a specialist and learned the distressing news—he was autistic.

Three phases of autism

In my work with children and ponies I see autism as passing through three stages:

1 The autistic phase when the child bonds with the pony but cuts himself off from the rest of the world.

2 The period of symbiosis in which the child extends the relationship with his pony to include me and his mother (it is vitally important that the mother is included at this point so that he accepts the idea that she will be part of everything new as he makes progress).

3 Finally, a stage when the child abandons his pony and runs about all over the place. As I have said, it is essential at this point to have him in a secure area and establish limits that he understands and accepts. If this is not done correctly he may have to be forcibly held, which you want to avoid. It may last a long time and can be very wearying. The child is slowly establishing his markers, something he cannot do if there is no limit to his environs. If he were to be surrounded by unlimited space he could never achieve the required understanding. (I will expand on these phases in the second half of this book—my journal—beginning on p. 125.)

I have spoken about anxiety shown in a social context. Christophe André and Patrick Légeron in their book *La Peur des Autres (The fear of others)* say that as a result of many studies it is generally accepted that apart from a genetic predisposition to autism that emerges from the moment the child is born and manifests itself in a strong reaction against any unaccustomed situation, autistic symptoms often show themselves about the age of two, first in the form of strange behavior, evolving into fear of social interaction, and ending in phobic behavior. According to Didier Houzel, this anxiety manifests itself in several forms: the fear of amputation, the fear of breakage, the fear of drowning, and the fear of explosion.

In most children these fears are gradually accommodated into a solid, permanent structure, what Frances Tustin calls the "the birth of the psyche," from about four months. This can be assisted by the calming effect of being walked on a pony, which helps to put the body axis into a good position.

In the case of an autistic child, the pony provides an even greater service. It helps to establish the feeling of the body's boundaries by the fact that it is in contact with so many parts of the child and is producing movement that enables him to build a mental image of his body as well as the realization that his body is different from the pony's—and, in the final analysis, another person's body. The pony serves first as a sort of nurse: it will probably be thought of as an extension of the child's self to begin with; then, the child invests the pony with human qualities because of their close connection. The feeling of total security and the confidence the pony engenders gradually allows the child's own separate identity to emerge.

Steven

Steven stroked my hair as if it were the pony's coat and then grabbed hold of my nose. I reacted by touching each part of his face while I named them: nose, eyes, and mouth. He mirrored my actions by touching all of mine in turn. Before this incident he would only go as far as touching the nose of Bubu, the clown, which is one of the toys in the small arena. When I made faces at Steven he mimicked them by grimacing at me.

After this episode Steven always responded to my facial expressions, and it was not long before we exchanged our first smile. When he tipped over one of the mounting blocks and some cones on purpose—to provoke me—I looked at him wide-eyed, and he understood my reaction, so much so that he continued to turn them over so that we could laugh. Subsequently, we enriched his emotional vocabulary: he understood when I had a cross or happy reaction and what caused these different states. I could be quite firm when necessary, and this enabled him to distinguish between my wishes and his. He also understood that I could transfer my wishes to him. Smiling and laughter are my constant companions: tears occasionally make their appearance, but I must always be on my guard not to allow anything that provokes fear.

This was all part of the process of Steven discovering "the other person." It is important for the teacher not to reject this game; it establishes a contact that might not otherwise be achieved.

Enriching the autistic child's education

When I began working with autistic children, their problems troubled me, but now that I have realized their amazing potential, I feel only joy and hope that I share with them. I find them fascinating, wonderfully sensitive, and responsive. Using my educational palette, I expose them to as many different objects, situations, and emotions as I can dream up, and watch them with joy and a feeling of achievement as their emotional and perceptive vocabulary grows. When a child smiles or makes a face, I imitate it. I often play a form of hide-and-seek by appearing and disappearing behind my outstretched hands and roaring with laughter when I meet their eyes again. Steven loves this particular game for which he uses his riding helmet, lowering it to cover his face and raising it suddenly with a shriek of joy.

This game of hide-and-seek is a great help in teaching about the permanence of "the other person," in that when the other is hidden, he does not disappear. A child's greatest fear is often that of being separated from his mother, something that takes place when the mother moves away from him. This is possibly to do with the fact that the child feels so close to his mother that he is part of her. Riding on the pony, it seems that the child also thinks of the pony as a part, or an an extension of himself, but separation does not produce the same effect. When it comes to leaving the pony, he is calling the tune, and the presence of the pony gives him the security he needs in order not to be anxious. This soon leads to his being able to move away from his mother and to come and go without anxiety.

With an autistic child something different happens: he will sometimes jump down from the saddle and run away as fast as he can. He then returns, roaring with laughter, but it can be an anxious moment for the teacher or the parent because of the risk of the child running into some danger. Catherine Mathelin-Vanier says that this strange behavior is not, as you might expect, in order to establish his own and separate identity but to experience the comfort and security of returning to the pony's protective presence.

Steven

In this respect Steven was particularly exhausting: he really gave me the runaround. One day I was going to fetch him where he was playing in the sandpit; he dropped the objects he was holding when he saw me approaching and began to charge around the pit, looking at me with a big smile on his face. I dropped into position beside him and imitated whatever he was doing. He stopped in astonishment, staring at me as if he'd never seen me before. I went up to him, took his hand, and we went over to the pony, which he mounted without hesitation by putting his foot in the stirrup.

This shows, I think, that Steven was aware by this time of "the other person" and secure in this knowledge. From that day on he never made me run after him again and accepted the limits I imposed on him as being also his own.

On another occasion Steven dismounted and headed for a big, blue plastic container that had been tipped on its side. He got into it, disappearing from view, and then reappeared; he repeated this game several times, both then and at future sessions, always looking at me intently. I called the game, "Now I see you, now I don't," and thought to myself how the container was exactly that: something that contained and gave him a feeling of security.

When Steven had been working with me for three years, I had a visit from Nathalie Durel, a French author and psychotherapist who lives in Portugal. She had bought my first book and had come to see me work.

To Nathalie, Steven did not, at this time, give the appearance of being autistic. At first sight he appeared to be a cheeky young lad full of the desire to do things and wanting to find out their limits— which was what I wanted of him at this stage. As an autistic child moves toward making relationships, he needs an adult to teach him where the boundaries are and give him markers. "It's essential for the adult to be aware of this need. That is what denotes a real therapist," Nicolas de Lahaye said to me.

I invited Nathalie to take charge of Steven. Nathalie, by the way, agrees with my belief that putting a child on a pony and setting off at a walk helps them to return to the very early moment in their existence when they were in or emerging from their mother's womb, and if possible, to set out anew from that point.

> *As soon as Nathalie took Steven over, he wanted to dismount. "The fact that a child wants to break away from a situation already demonstrates a certain security," Nathalie told me. Steven did not know Natalie so he was reluctant to accept her as an authority and after dismounting rushed over to me for a cuddle, but interestingly, it was he who was cuddling me and not the reverse. At that moment, his mother came up to us, and Steven extended his embrace to include her.*

After this performance, he agreed to remount at Nathalie's request and by so doing, Nathalie explained, he was awarding himself the right to make his own decisions and thereby going beyond the limits he had hitherto established. The pony was still the mediator, the safety blanket, in a way the extension of himself—a living being that made no demands, allowing him to establish a relationship with me, who he thought of as an extension of the pony. When Steven became aware of this he no longer had to go to the pony first before coming to me. We were inextricably connected so he could come directly to me.

Nathalie watched me working for a whole week: she had been captivated by my first book and helped me to understand this very tricky question of transferring confidence first to an animal and then to a person. Her visit convinced me even more, if that were necessary, of the importance of my role in accompanying my riders as they progressed.

LANGUAGE

"An autistic person has difficulty in regulating the tone of his voice, which is usually rather high-pitched and monotonous in character. His relationship to sound is complicated and probably has its roots in some experience even before he was born. He is hypersensitive to certain noises (any machinery that vibrates, such as a drill or a lawnmower) but also to hard speech consonants," writes Genevieve Haag, a French psychoanalyst with a special knowledge of childhood autism.

A horse breathes audibly and neighs. Language requires breath that comes from the diaphragm and gives birth to sounds. Seated on the back of the pony, the autistic child is conscious of sounds and vibrations to which he begins to respond. As I walk along beside him I name the objects we see, taking care always to use the same word. The child then echoes what I have said; I use exactly the same technique that I learned with my "baby riders."

"Echolalia (automatic repetition), once considered an aberration that should be suppressed, is an important step for an autistic person: it represents an effort by them to communicate when they find normal language too difficult to master," says Theo Peeters.

Lucien

When he was seven, Lucien had been with me for over two years. By this time he was speaking clearly. For instance, on Thursday he said, "Mommy phoned me and she is coming here tomorrow." On Friday I said to him, "So Mommy is coming today," to which he replied, "No, it's tomorrow. She told me tomorrow."

I explained to him that yesterday we would have spoken about today as "tomorrow," but since then we'd all been to sleep and the day had changed, it was a new day—"today."

"No," he repeated, "Mommy said tomorrow." At this point I didn't insist, but as he was leaving, I nevertheless reminded him that his Mommy was coming "today."

The five young riders I had been working with were chatting together. Lucien was the eldest. Steven was bursting with newly acquired vocabulary and giving names to objects and feelings.

The importance of starting to speak by age seven

On the subject of speech, Donald Meltzer says, "The prolonged immaturity of autistic children tends to take them past the period when children are most rapidly acquiring their language skills, one that usually begins to dry up after the age of seven. Children who cannot speak by that age have a huge handicap."

This is all the more reason to start as early as possible. I have noticed that in order to teach children to speak, you have to combine emotion, the object, gesture and the words with great sensitivity. Autistic children are very aware of our emotional state so I take great care to stay calm, smile when possible and use a melodious voice. Daniel Tammet speaks about how difficult it is to filter noises from the outside and says he regularly put his hands to his ears in order to be able to concentrate.

We build up our visual universe often with connected sounds and for most of us this learning is automatic, gradual, and without accompanying stress. But, according to Michel Lemay, autistic people do not acquire their "sound" envelope with such ease (see p. 57). Some sounds are difficult for them to accept and may cause stress; associations of sound and touch or sound and sight may also be a source of difficulty. What is easy for us is almost certainly difficult for them, so I have made of point of putting aside all my preconceptions, and I try to discover everything that might be of help to them.

WORDS

As we all know, words can mean many things when used in different ways and contexts. Subtleties of meaning are conveyed often by the tone of voice. Used in an ironic sense, words can mean the opposite of their normal meaning. An autistic child, however, learns the meaning of a word and then takes it literally, so it is essential, at least at first, not to confuse them and be as straightforward as you can in the choice of words.

Even though an object has more than one word to describe it, I take care to use only one at first. In the same way I make sure to use the same object for each game we play. For instance, when we are transferring a colored ball from one basket to another I make a note of which color we use and remember to use that same one on the next occasion. I give great importance to gestures, but here again, I try to use the same gesture each time I employ it to indicate an action or object.

Robert

The hazards of being too free with words were brought home to me when I saw two-year-old Robert squinting at the sun and I said to him, "The sun is in your eyes."He immediately replied, "The sun is in the sky." Later on, he pointed at the sun and said, "Eyes!"

Fortunately, the horse world comes to our aid in this respect as well. Every action taken in riding, each piece of equipment, has a specific name: walk, trot, canter, stirrups, saddle, and so forth. Also, in the matter of noise that disturbs the autistic person, the pony or horse is there to help. I noticed, for instance, that Steven listened most attentively to the pony's breathing, but when it neighed, the little boy nearly jumped out of his skin. Steven emitted his first sounds very reluctantly, and I think the pony's breathing and neighing were a big help in giving him the idea that sounds came out from somewhere inside us and are associated with breath.

Steven

I remember one session early on when Steven had been silent for a long time. I said to him, "Steven, you haven't said a word for ages." He replied by saying, "Bravo!" a word that I had been using repeatedly during the day because he had been doing so well.

There is an Argentinian doctor in Cordoba who has proposed the theory that the very act of riding has an indirect effect on a person's jaw, specifically the bones near the base of the tongue, and possibly parts of the brain, because of the rhythmical motion of the horse that affects the whole human frame as it is passed right through the rider's body and into the head. It is not only autistic people who benefit from this phenomenon but brain-damaged people, too.

Not uncommonly, my little autistic riders will, in the middle of a session, give vent to a cacophony of sounds that resemble babbling—rather like babies. This gives way in the course of time to words and then to phrases that describe actions and objects. I am constantly using these words and phrases combined with gestures that elucidate their meaning, and when the children begin to use them themselves, I know we are making progress. Finally, they take the step of using these words and phrases in new contexts.

Steven

On the cover of the French edition of this book is a picture of me with Steven and his pony. In addition to the three of us and the photographer, his mother and the book editor were also there. While preparing to shoot this I had to ask Steven to ride his pony alone in the large area outside the building, which made us all a little nervous. He had never been on his own in that area, and it was not contained like the indoor arenas. At a certain point he dismounted and was reluctant to get back on the pony. I explained to him that we were taking photographs and asked him to remount. He replied, "Wait a moment," an expression I often use with him when we are changing a procedure.

SYMBOLISM AND THE IMAGINARY

I try to deal with difficult situations by playing games that draw on symbolism and imaginary elements. Autistic children have great difficulty in facing up to their fears: they do not have the intellectual tools to identify and describe them so that they can deal with them. I invent all sorts of stories, some involving dragons and dinosaurs that the child feels strong enough on horseback to face. These children do actually believe in the existence of the invented creatures, and Catherine Mathelin-Vanier advises that the right approach is to abandon the real and return to the imaginary. This is the exact opposite of the usual analytic approach to curing neurotic problems by helping the person to abandon his imaginary fears and enter the real world.

Lucien

Lucien always has a little plastic sword with him so he can attack and defeat the wild beasts that fill his imagination. I said to him, "With that sword and on horseback, Lucien, you need fear nothing. You are a proper knight. "No," he replied, "I am Lucien."

At this point Lucien was not able to enter into the spirit of the game to the extent that he could assume another personage. He couldn't be someone else or use his toys as pretend weapons. To him the sword was as real as the fears that populated his imagination. When he left to attack the dinosaurs, they were there; they were absolutely real to him. "For real" and "for play" was not a distinction that he could grasp and it brought home to me the quality of terror that these children suffer.

Yet I could use the idea of magic with him to good effect. My pony club arena is, as I have described, in a wooded area. Around its perimeter are large letters that are used for dressage work; I told Lucien that these were magic letters: for instance, I said that the M stood for "Mommy" to which he replied excitedly, "I'll tell her." When we went into the woods to do battle with dinosaurs and dragons we always passed by these magic letters.

Lucien rode with me from the age of two-and-a-half. He is now seven and has acquired a good level of language skills. His vocabulary is impressive. He eventually reached the point at which he accepted that our battles with these terrifying creatures was a kind of game. On the day this happened, I gave him a new, big, plastic sword that would bend, and we had a game with the other kids, or rather "knights." They accepted the rules that were most precise: they could only be knights when on horseback; the limits of the play area could not be surpassed; they could only strike another person's sword, not his body or the pony. (It was at about this time that Lucien pointed out his pony's name above his stall: Figaro. He had grasped what the words represented.)

Our rides in the woods are also filled with images. I tell the children that we will not encounter any dragons or dinosaurs because they are frightened of ponies, particularly when ridden by knights. Wolves are another source of fear, and here I employ the use of magic again; wolves cannot abide ponies ridden by young knights!

THE FIRST SIGNS OF INTERACTION

As I've described, the first thing I do with my little riders is tour the space and establish markers that define our surroundings; these may consist of objects lying about or parts of the building. If their attention is still wholly absorbed by one of their "autistic objects," I focus my own attention on an object so that the child sees we are working together. I look at an object, and I touch it or pick it up. This is already a progression, combining sight and touch.

I stay close but not too close to my young rider, and I do not make demands, such as trying to look him in the eye. At this stage his vision is normally focusing on the periphery of the space we are in rather than on a particular object. I do not try to establish relations with him, and I leave a space between us for him to slip into when he feels confident enough to do so.

The surroundings of the pony club are so full of interesting items, smells, sounds, and sights that they are a rich experience and provide a stepping-stone to communication. My objective is to inspire the children to begin exploring for themselves: they familiarize themselves with everything that can be seen, touched, smelled, and watched. They go where they want and learn to cope with the unexpected. Soon, I find, they have the desire to share an experience and that is the start of communication.

Imitation does not require language, but it is still communication
I do not at first make any demands. I make gestures by pointing things out and perhaps naming them—always using the same word and calm intonation, or I touch something without looking for a reaction. However, in the

way in which the children respond to what I do, I can learn something about them: I can see if they look quickly away or follow what I am doing with a spark of interest. As the child becomes more confident, I often find that he starts imitating what I do: I touch an object and then he touches it; I look at something and he follows the direction of my gaze. Should he attempt to repeat the word I have used, I know we are making progress. Imitation is the way in which an autistic child forges his personality.

While this sort of activity is in progress, the child is moving along on horseback, which is unconsciously helping by making him adjust and balance his body. As we have seen, a proper body axis is essential to put in place before a full range of movements are possible: he can turn to the right or the left, look up at the rafters or the colorful balls that are suspended at specific heights, or lean forward and look at the ground.

Fortunately, autistic children are brilliant imitators once they get the hang of it. They love imitating facial expressions, so I have to remain very conscious of the emotions I am displaying with my face.

I am also most careful not to do anything too complicated to start with: I stick with simple, repeated gestures so that imitation is easy for them. Once a movement is mastered I can progress slowly to something more complicated. I think one has to treat autistic children very gently, in the same way that you would treat a baby. I can easily repeat an action ten times or even more until a child is completely at home with what I have repeated and does it himself.

An autistic person needs extra time to take in, sort, analyze, and add new information to their understanding

Learning appears to take place for all of us in two stages. The first stage is more like imitation, but by the second stage we absorb the new experience into what we already know and thereby expand our knowledge base. It must be appreciated that it takes a little longer for an autistic child to complete the second stage, so you need patience.

Since the pony club is packed with objects of every size, color, and shape: big balloons, rings, small play balls, toy ducks, frogs, fishes, and jungle animals, all these objects and creatures have to become familiar to the children and be fitted into their overall picture of the club. If they need an "autistic object" at an early stage when they easily lose confidence and retreat into a state of handling this item in a repetitive manner, they can choose whatever they want. I make no suggestions and impose no limits.

In the quest for communication, body language comes long before speech. This is why it is so important to get a child's body axis sorted out. The act of riding soon produces improvement so that the child can express himself with all kinds of bodily movements and gestures that would not at first be possible—and then he can imitate more easily. Once there is an awareness of the connection between hand and vision, I introduce him to the act of giving and receiving. For this I often make use of my "baby riders." When a baby cries, I find an autistic child can be very attentive, reaching out toward the baby with his hand, though often he has seen other children doing this, so there is a degree of imitation. The baby may point at things he wants, and this helps to establish communication between them.

Steven

> Once, on a hot day, Steven asked for water by simply saying, "Water." I fetched five glasses of water—there were five children in the group—and handed them out to the other four, momentarily keeping back Steven's glass. It was not long before he said, "Me," even though the pronunciation was incorrect. Of course, I immediately gave him his glass and then worked with the concept of "For me" and "For you."

Once I have discovered a child's favorite object—the one he retreats to playing with in moments of stress—I might pick it up and hold it in front of his eyes. If I lower the brim of his riding helmet the object disappears. Then I raise it, and there it is again. The child is probably intrigued by this point, and we all burst into laughter. We have done something together, we have laughed together; soon a verbal relationship will follow.

Language replaces actions and objects with words

The autistic child is surprisingly observant and possesses an excellent visual memory that helps when the recovery process begins. Images and feelings still make up important markers for the child as they do for the helper and are remembered easily. Sound traces are more complex because they disappear more quickly, and in order to remain, they have to be repeated many times in the same context.

I make sure that words always accompany actions so that little by little they can be used to describe objects that are not present, as well as intended actions. The symbolic quality of words in a sense replaces the object. The mastery of language comes about through sensory and visual experiences.

As Bernard Golse, a pediatrician, child psychiatrist, and author says, the ability to think does not arrive on a plate; it is a product of our experiences and how we interpret or register them in our understanding.

This is where the pony is such a help: it provides a constant source of new—and repeated—experiences; it automatically improves the posture of the autistic child and this produces a completely new range of feelings. It enables the child to be more adventurous and explore areas he had never dared to before. By having to reach for objects as he goes along the child improves his physical ability and his strength, which lead to an improvement in his feeling of well-being. There are other children on ponies so he has, of necessity, to take their presence into account and control the direction he goes. This is the beginning of social behavior and interaction. In addition, he cannot help but observe the other children and may well want to imitate some of the actions he sees.

All in all you can understand how the child develops a sense of his own body that leads to his acknowledging new sensations and the growth of thought processes. It should also be pointed out that his experiences are enjoyable, and since they are constantly repeated, so is the pleasure that he derives from them.

Needless to say, this period of growth is very demanding both on the child and the teacher. The child has to make huge efforts and can be very tired as a result. I also become exhausted because I am so involved with each child and live through their experiences as though I myself were having them. I establish the closest imaginable contact with these kids and find myself part of their hypersensitive world. I know I am always learning from them as I become ever more receptive to their feelings and more attuned to the significance of their gestures and facial expressions. When their behavior takes an unexpected turn, I have to be prepared for it and know how to cope.

Steven

Steven reached the stage when he would suddenly jump off his pony and take off. I reckoned he was asking to have limits established that he could understand and accept. It was also, perhaps, a gesture of defiance of authority. When he did this on one occasion in the woods, I had to run and catch him, but all the time, he was laughing and enjoying the adventure. I finally caught him and we walked for a while, hand in hand. But then, when he tried the same thing again, I simply said, "Steven, you should not run away like that." He stopped doing it: he had accepted the new parameters I set him.

Ernest

At one point Ernest came up to me, and pointing at me with his finger said, "You!" Later on he said, "Wednesday!" and then lastly, "Horse!" These were all things associated with his time at the pony club. Finally, he called me correctly by my first name.

chapter 9

The Freeing of Emotions

"The children have to take notice of the pony's pattern of movement in order to adjust their body position and balance and to organize their own gestures. Through stimulation of the sensory receptors in their muscles and tendons, they discover and experience entirely new sensations and perceptions, generated entirely by being on horseback."
—Hubert Montagner

A n autistic child cannot rid himself of his emotions in the way a baby can. He lives them more intensely so they stay around much longer. A very young baby needs his mother during the first months of his existence to surround him with love and security, to wipe away his fears when things seem to go wrong. Later on he is able to confide in an adult he trusts and again overcome his fears and doubts.

The autistic child does not have this ability: he has no means of accepting outside stimuli and no confidence in the people who have contact with him. He cannot confide in anyone, and in order not to collapse altogether he tries to protect himself from the outside world by retreating into his shell.

D.W. Winnicott lists some of the primitive and disquieting fears of an autistic child. Among these are the fear of returning to a state where he is disconnected from anything around him; the fear of falling through space; and the fear that he will not be able to have any proper relationship with an object. His responses to these fears are to disintegrate, to lock himself into his "prison," and to use "autistic objects" in a meaningless, repetitive manner.

Catherine Mathelin-Vanier says we have to allow or encourage the autistic child to put words to his fears—those things he has so far refused to face or to formulate. Temple Grandin says that in her experience, the more she allowed herself to play out her fears and emotions, the more she understood what other people were going through, and this helped her begin to feel compassion.

Steven

Steven went with his family to visit an uncle in Paris. The journey and the days passed uneventfully, but come the nights, he began to scream and cry. His mother told me about this the next time we met, and she reckoned it was caused by Steven returning to a very early moment in his existence when, toward bedtime, a child cries for his mother to feed him.

This observation made me think about how truly archaic the fears are of these autistic children, and also how closely involved they are with their mother. It brought home to me the importance of involving the mother at every stage of the therapeutic work I do. Whatever happens I must not leave the mother to face these tragic events alone, and in fact, I keep them well informed of everything that is going on; we confide in each other and share our anxieties as well as our triumphs and our experiences. They give me the benefit of their own discoveries and the result is that I build a close relationship with them as I do with the child.

Some months later, Steven was taking part in a session that ended in the dark. His mother reminded me that he was frightened of the dark, so I looked at him and said, "Steven, I know you are a little frightened of the dark, but if you like, we could go for a walk together because I'm not frightened of it at all." Steven took my hand, and we set off into the dark.

My role is to reassure and help the child face his fears. He was in this instance able to listen to his fears being described, subsequently to share them with me and thus overcome them.

Some weeks later, Steven suddenly broke down in tears; it was the first time I had seen him in such a state; he was inconsolable. I failed to comfort him and so did the pony. I tried putting him with other children, but this also didn't work to stem the flood of tears. Steven's mother had no choice but to take him home. I said goodbye and told him I knew he was sad and that I would see him soon again.

It must be said that I was quite depressed at having to part from Steven in this condition, so I tried to work out what could possibly have caused it. I came up with a number of possibilities:

- Our session had taken place rather late in the evening when night was falling.
- I was making too great a demand on Steven with regard to language because he had been making such good progress recently.
- His mother told me that he'd had rather a difficult visit to the hospital.
- Something unexplained was taking place inside him.

I discussed the problem with Nicolas de Lahaye who said not to worry: a crisis like this is all part of the evolution toward "normality." He said that I had to remain strong and reassuring and it would pass. He was right.

In fact, at the time of this incident, Steven was in a good frame of mind with everyone and his language ability had just made a further leap.

Donald Meltzer remarks that autistic children have raw, unprotected psyches that are vulnerable to every breeze. Denys Ribas adds, "This absence of any protection exposes the children to the equivalent of an emotional bombardment in which they are too aware of another person's pain. In this respect they are like babies and can be aware of other people's emotions, but this cannot be taken as an indication that they know who they themselves are or who the other person is. At this stage there is no proper distinction in their minds between themselves and someone else."

I think we have to return to a primitive moment in the child's life, one when it is too early to *even think* about knowing who he is, so we can first remove his anxieties, and then allow him to make a fresh start. This is what the pony does together with my help and commitment: it allows emotions to be liberated, right from the gentle rocking produced by walking, to the strong outside stimulus produced at the canter. The pony and I absorb the worries and give the children the confidence they need to step out again into the world: they dare to learn, to acknowledge the existence of others, and accept their own unique individuality.

> *Speaking of cantering, I remember an occasion when Steven was four years old and had only been with me for a year. He jumped off his pony at a canter, without falling, and ran over to bury his head in his mother's embrace. It was like watching a cat, such was his dexterity.*

Three of my little charges have similarly demanded cuddles for the first time at three or four years old, and these cuddles sparked the beginning of an affectionate relationship with their mother—and by extension with me. I also get cuddles!

> *The following August when everyone was on vacation, Steven's mother phoned me to say that he was going through a very difficult period: he watched out of the window for cars passing by, and when they failed to stop, he became agitated. I suggested that even though it was holiday time, she bring him to the pony club for special lessons. After only a short time, this had the effect of calming him down, and to my delight, he began to cuddle me. Before this time, he had resisted any affectionate contact by going rigid when I put my arms around him. I considered this a significant moment in Steven's life, recognizing that he needed another person as protector.*

Understanding horses

In a strange way, I see a connection between horses and autistic people at the primitive stage of their development. In the wild state a horse is potential prey to stronger animals. It is a gregarious animal and the herd affords some protection, but it has to be constantly on guard and ready to take flight. Any circumstance the horse perceives as threatening or unsettling can provoke violent and unexpected reactions, including phobic and stereotypical behavior patterns. I need hardly point out the similarity to autistic children.

Appreciating these qualities, I spend hours with my ponies and young horses, and as a result, I have grown very close to them and feel I understand how their minds work. A small incident—one we humans would hardly notice—can trigger the flight instinct, just like with an autistic child, and I take infinite pains to avoid any phobic behavior becoming established. Once a phobia is established, it is extremely difficult to get rid of it. I have worked in stables where horses grind their teeth or rock from side to side—both behavior patterns that denote an environment where something is very wrong.

You have to desensitize autistic children slowly

Unlike children, horses, soon after birth, are independent enough to have a strong instinct of survival through their own efforts. Children, however, need the support of their mother, parents, or other protectors for years before they can strike out on their own. It is neatly put by Ashley Montagu in his book *Touching: The Human Significance of the Skin,* where he asks why it is that humans are born in such a state of immaturity, so much so that they need eight to ten months to crawl and another four to six months before they walk and talk. And, it takes even more years before they can subsist on their own without the help and support of others. There is no other animal that takes so long to become self-sufficient. In the meantime, the human goes through periods marked by anxiety and lack of self-confidence.

In the case of autistic children, anxiety can be triggered by the smallest change in the environment, one that a normal person might not even notice. Likewise, there could be some emotional problem among those surrounding him that is enough to cause a crisis. Often this is in the form of furious temper tantrums that I interpret as cries for help and a desperate need for relationships that they have so far found impossible to forge. They have retreated into a world of their own in which they exist with their mix of psychotic characteristics, their high intelligence, and their oversensitivity. They find themselves apart and strangely self-sufficient, but terrified of what is, or might be, found outside.

I remember an incident with a little child of two-and-a-half. His parents insisted that he say "please" when he asked me for something. He didn't react, and when the parents repeated their demand, he flew into a temper, resulting in the parents getting angry as well. I went up to the little fellow and said, "Don't worry, give me a kiss and that will do. He did as I had suggested and then said to me, "I can't." "Can't say, please?" I asked. "Yes!" he replied.

This is an example of parents causing unnecessary anxiety through lack of understanding. Unfortunately, those living with autistic children or charged with their care are often guilty of similarly unhelpful behavior, which acts like indigestible food and prevents the formation of any kind of helpful relationship because it does not engender a state of confidence.

It's so different when you see my "baby riders" watching the riding sessions and putting in place a stable emotional relationship with the ponies and with me: their eyes are wide open, they frequently smile and perhaps wave their arms and legs to show how they are connecting with me and the ponies. Their faces and gestures tell all. They are interacting with other people, animals, and with their environment.

It can be the same thing with the autistic children when they find themselves in surroundings that are reassuring, where no one makes demands, in which they find they can communicate with ponies and with a pony/person, and then with each other. No one is telling them they have to say "please"!

THE ENVIRONMENT MUST ADAPT, NOT THE CHILD

Steven

When Steven was four, his parents sent him to a nursery school twice a week for two hours. No special arrangements had been made to deal with him so it was a disaster from the start. Steven became ever more agitated: he screamed and cried with the result that it was highly disruptive for the other children. The teachers had no experience or training in dealing with a child like Steven so the situation rapidly escalated from bad to worse.

At this point Steven's mother got in touch with me. She told me what was happening and added that when Steven got home he was much more agitated than usual. I was invited to come to a meeting, and as a result, Steven came to my pony club for therapeutic riding sessions four times a week. His mother understood that a normal school environment was not suitable for Steven at this stage and that it would only lead to chaos and increased anxiety. One simply had to accept that an autistic child has his own requirements, which are like those of a baby who has not been able to start the process of building himself into a full person.

Marie-Françoise Livoir-Petersen describes the autistic syndrome as one that resembles the effect of the child and his family being inundated by a cascade of unimaginably awful events.

In contrast, Professor Montagner talks about the first three years in the life of a child without autism—whatever his environment. A normal child will learn to cope with the six emotional states considered to be innate and universal: joy, anger, fear, sadness, surprise, and confidence. An autistic child does not cope, although contact with the pony begins to make this possible. Where humans, in spite of all the impressive medical advances cannot find a way, the pony, a veritable ball of feelings and primitive but reassuring qualities can. With the help of the pony—and the feeling that the child has of being an extension of the pony, just as he thinks of me as half pony and half person—he can, for the first time, give vent to his emotions and establish relationships with others.

Patrick Ben Soussan, a child psychiatrist especially interested in very young babies and author of *Le Bébé et Ses Peurs* (The baby's fears), explores the myriad components that a child has to put in place in order to build a good emotional self. For all children it is a precarious business, and he considers they are always hovering on the edge of anxiety that we can hardly fathom.

In his first year, a baby has to recognize, classify, and name things; make sense of his environment and discover his place in it. First, he is aware of the people that inhabit his world; at about three to six months he begins to be able to express emotions like laughter, anger, fear, and at about two years old, shame and envy. Then come the "motor–learning" skills: he starts to understand the effects of crying, gestures, body positions, imitates what he observes. And, a decision has to be made about collapsing in a heap in face of a threat, or fleeing to safety, instead.

I enter their world and we share joyful times

The point Soussan is making is that even when children have all their faculties functioning normally, it is an incredible achievement to absorb all the information and lessons of the early months and years. Just imagine how disadvantaged a child is who has decided to retreat behind a brick wall. He is so fearful of facial expressions, voices, noises, and of being separated from the person he trusts, that no progress is made until I return him, with the help of the pony, to the moment when he "closed down" and we can make a fresh start. He allows access to his emotions and, as a result, he can liberate them.

As for me, I enter his strange world and share with him the adventure of learning to feel, to love, to hate, even to seek protection when he meets a danger. I share his laughter—as, for instance, on the occasion I play hide-and-seek with Steven by lowering and raising his riding helmet—and his tears. We bond, and this bonding is a necessary part in his efforts to rebuild himself, have rational thoughts, and display emotion when he needs to.

Whereas formerly the only emotion they have allowed themselves is anxiety, there are now wonderful sensations to be enjoyed, like the rocking of the pony that reminds them of the time when all was still well, and the pleasurable adventures of friendship, laughter, and love. It is vitally important to keep these new emotions and avoid in every possible way anything that makes the children fearful. In the early life of any child, of course he will experience fear, but the key is to be able to express this, which an autistic child cannot; he sublimates fear and it festers, adding to the damage already done.

How can I describe the debt I owe to the ponies? They seem to enter into the spirit of what I am trying to achieve; not many people might agree with me, but I sometimes feel that they really understand what is going on and do their best to help. Sometimes they have to endure chaos and aggression when an autistic child loses control, but even in these rare moments they are patient and appear to understand.

Maurice

One day we had an unfortunate incident with an autistic adult who was twenty-five years old. Maurice had been diagnosed at the age of twelve but had only been coming to us for a year. The teacher, Catherine, was taking the class. She put Maurice in the middle of the sand-pit area with some other riders while she got another group to canter. Seeing what was taking place, Maurice tried to imitate the action of cantering, though what, in fact, he was imitating was the rising trot. He became very frustrated and when the group that had been cantering came to a stop, he tried first to hit them, and then he struck his own horse. Catherine intervened and told him that if he continued he would have to dismount, which he immediately did and started striking his own face. Catherine said quite calmly, "Maurice, you can mount your horse now but be kind to him as well as to your friends." Maurice got back in the saddle and calmed down.

It was an instructive incident. Prior to it, Maurice had been sitting on his horse sucking one of his thumbs and holding a page of a magazine between his other thumb and forefinger. After the incident, he adopted a good position in the saddle and shortly after, abandoned the paper, took his thumb out of his mouth, and turned toward his group; the anger had evaporated.

In spite of all the advances in understanding I feel I have made, I see that I am still faced with masses of questions and a sea of unknowing. But there has been real progress and the ponies are very much part of it.

chapter 10

Family, Friends, and Caregivers

"During all her years of psychotherapy, it was love that seemed to be most important to Temple. It was as though to compensate for all the early years in which she could neither give love nor accept it, she is only happy now when she feels she is loved."
—Temple Grandin's mother in a letter to the child psychiatrist quoted in Grandin's book *Thinking in Pictures: My Life with Autism*

Frances Tustin points out that when a child turns out to be autistic, he is trapped with his mother in a chain of physical and mental reactions from which there seems no escape and that when we try to help, we must not give the poor parents, who have suffered so much already, false hope that a cure will be easy. It is vitally important to give support to the family and to explain to them that it may take years, during which they will have to show exemplary strength and accept that advances are often infinitesimally small. Sometimes they will feel that there is no light at the end of the tunnel.

It is the duty of therapists, says Pierre Delion, a psychiatrist who has expressed strong disapproval of aspects of psychiatric intervention in France, especially in relation to asylums, to put in place a framework that includes the care of the family members and friends who are responsible for the child. They have to be supported, given helpful advice, and occasionally revived when the job overwhelms them.

Nicolas de Lahaye, when writing about my work, makes it clear that I do include the parents and caregivers, and make no demands on them; this has the effect of involving them even more closely. They soon notice that I begin by watching their child without making judgments, and this helps them to sharpen their own observational skills. I find that the more they watch what I am doing, the closer it brings them to their child and opens their mind to new ideas and feelings. It also allows them to get to know other parents, similarly burdened, to exchange thoughts and ideas, and often to put in place a strong mutual support group that has the same interests and hopes at heart. Parents frequently come in pairs and not infrequently with the grandparents. Sometimes our excursions into the woods resemble processions, there are so many of the family present.

I can't help overhearing what people talk about, and it can often be of help to know what they think. The beneficial effects of contact with the pony are all too evident, but the reasons why this should be so is in some senses clothed in mystery and open to question. It is fascinating for me to hear what people make of it and I have been listening to the comments of friends and family for over 30 years.

Elise

Here is what happened one day as described by a child's mother: "My daughter Elise was three months old and accepted very little food, and then, only with difficulty; we even had to hospitalize her. On this after-noon, I took her with me to watch her three-year-old brother having his riding lesson. I sat her on my knees watching the proceedings, and to my surprise (because she never showed any interest in what was going on around her) she began to wave her arms.

"Claudine, as always very focused on her riders, also kept an eye open to what was happening on the sideline, and she noticed this ani-mated display. She came up to Elise and said, 'Would you like to have a little ride with your brother?' Without considering what I was doing, I handed Elise to Claudine. Of course, I was anxious about her, but I had been given a grain of hope by seeing her animated response. Once

in the saddle with her brother and safely held in position by Claudine she broke into a smile. This was undoubtedly a key moment in her life— when we returned home she ate normally and we did not have to take her back to hospital."

Another parent invited one of her friends whose twenty-month-old baby Olivier woke his parents a dozen times during the night. Standard medical help had not had any beneficial effect, but after only two sessions at the pony club, the child recovered his composure and the parents slept well again. I do not in any way pretend there is anything magic about all this: I am only giving the parents the chance to withdraw a little and to start afresh.

Nicolas de Lahaye describes what I do as making a game of relationships in which a bit of space allows each person to play their part vis-à-vis the other. I was merely answering Elise's yearning and giving Olivier a little outing on a pony. The parents trust me enough to take their children and put some distance between them and their child. They are able to watch everything, and they seem to know that this temporary separation will in some way help them. When Olivier first came with his parents, their faces were marked by the strain of sleepless nights and their anxiety at the cause of this behavior. It only needed the pony, with its comforting rocking motion, to absorb Olivier's primitive anxiety that might have been caused by fear of the dark or separation—who knows? I certainly do not, but what does it matter? The pony gave the boy strength and peace, and the troubles vanished.

After the event I spoke to the parents as I always do. I told them I was no magician: for me it is a matter of respecting each person's role. The parents showed confidence in me and so we forged an instant bond. The child was aware of this; there was no forcing of any kind. My only motive was to come to the aid of a little child that was disrupting his family and creating a situation that was spiraling out of control: the parents exhausted and anxious, not knowing what to do. At that point, I and my ponies were the intermediaries that enabled them to break out of the trap, to give each one back the space they needed.

I described this idea of necessary cooperation to Elise's parents by saying, "Elise wanted something; I understood what she wanted and put her on the pony; you had confidence in me and knew what you had to do. Elise relied on everyone involved: you, her mother, who trusted me; the pony that took her into its care; and me, because I was accompanying her."

Ophelia

Ophelia was in full crisis at eight months old. I made a plan with her parents: First, we put Ophelia in the saddle with her mother holding her. As soon as the baby caught my eye, she burst into tears, so I immediately looked away. For the second session, I arranged for her father to hold her in the saddle, and I noticed that from time to time she glanced at me. At the third session Ophelia gave me a broad smile, let go of her mother and made it clear that she wanted another ride on the pony. This time I took her and there was no further problem.

Each of the preceding examples, in my opinion, touches on the primitive fears that inhabit the mind of autistic children. Because there was no communication, these anxieties could not be dealt with and thus removed. It is not for me to say why the links of communication were not forged. It was not long before I could say to Olivier's family, "Maybe your son was frightened of being separated from you, or perhaps it was fear of the dark. But the fact is, thanks to the pony, each one of you was able to make a bit of distance between each other and start again. It's not a big deal: just a little distance that can and did, in this case, trigger a new beginning."

Luigi

Luigi's parents had tried everything imaginable to help their little boy when he was diagnosed with autism at eighteen months. They had taken him to a child psychiatrist then, and again, at the age of two-and-a-half. Both doctors had diagnosed depression associated with problems of nursing.

Luigi had been Catherine Mathelin-Vanier's patient when she brought him and his parents to see me. They were all smiling when they arrived and there was a confident, optimistic atmosphere that affected us all. I took Luigi in my arms, placed him on the pony and set off. Later his father told me, "We were really surprised by this instantaneous action that took place without any preamble. Luigi is usually frightened of strangers and any form of contact, so we were expecting him to start crying, but you just put him in the saddle and set off, while at the same time, you put his helmet on. Usually, he hates anything on his head so it must have been the direct effect of the pony's motion that brought him confidence and which he associated with you."

> *On that first occasion, I was the pony/lady to Luigi. These first moments are so delicate that I usually say nothing, though, this time, I turned back to the parents and invited them to come with us. "Surely we ought to stay here while he moves away from us a little?" his mother said confidently. (Later on his father said how valuable and restorative it was for them to have a few minutes to themselves.) Luigi was more relaxed by the minute as the pony's gentle movement rocked him. When we approached the edge of the woods, Luigi let out a shriek, so I immediately turned back to the open area where the arena is, and after waiting fifteen minutes, we returned to the arena. I sat on the edge as Luigi explored part of the area on foot, seemingly conscious of the safety perimeter around it. After another quarter-hour, when he had been happily sitting on the ground about two yards away from me, we returned to his parents, who were rewarded with a smile from Luigi.*

As a result of what they saw that day Luigi's parents rented an apartment near the pony club and came every day for two weeks. I had a lot of contact with the parents who kept me in touch with Luigi's phenomenal progress. "Within five days he stopped messing himself, probably as a result of watching ponies urinate and defecate," they told me. It was, at that point, that the first fears emerged. This is an important moment in the treatment because it enables me to give a palatable shape to the fear.

It turned out that Luigi was terrified of tomatoes! Earlier in the book (see p. 47) I related how there happened to be some tomato plants grow-ing near where I live, so we were able to visit them every day until he became accustomed to them. I would always pick one, turn it around in my hand and hand it to his mother, making sure that Luigi was paying attention. After a few days repeating these actions, I handed a tomato to Luigi, which he threw on the ground. However, the next day when I did the same thing again, he kept hold of it. Ever since that day, Luigi gladly ate tomatoes and even began to broaden the variety of things he would eat.

He babbled a lot at first, employing the new words that I used to describe all the goings-on at the pony club, the natural world around us, and the games we played together, but gradually he gained confidence and his little body showed the change clearly. As soon as he expressed a fear and dealt with it, he began to register all sorts of motor and emo-tional experiences. He very quickly understood the parts of his body that influenced the pony's action; within a short time we were noticing things together, sharing experiences, and chattering to each other. I often follow that progression: observing, discovering, experiencing, and then putting words to what has been happening. Words begin to make sense.

I was very touched by what Luigi's parents said to me: "Having confi-dence in another person allowed him to look at the world around him and to start living in it. We can tell when someone believes in Luigi and has confidence in him. It made all the difference. Gradually he took control of his body, and it was as if he decided what form that body was going to assume. Look at him now: he runs like an athlete, he is fully aware of the space around him and all the plants and trees that you have taught him to smell and recognize. Every time he comes home our car looks like a forest inside because of all the leaves and branches he has collected."

Nowadays, Luigi's family comes to see me every week and even take their holidays in the area. Luigi's baby brother, Edgardo, began riding at twelve months and adores coming here; their car journey from Paris and back is full of singing and laughter, the parents tell me.

Here are parents who trusted my original approach to dealing with an autistic child. Confidence led to friendship and the shared conviction that a child should not be seen as either "normal" or "handicapped." Each child is unique and pursues his own special way. Luigi's mother said to me that when they accepted this it helped them to grow. In the course of one year Luigi made considerable progress; he was an engaging little rascal!

> *I remember one occasion when we dismounted in a clearing in the woods and I encouraged him to blow dandelion heads. He imitated me but seemed upset by the seeds detaching themselves and touching his face as they floated away on the air. He came up to me holding a dandelion and removed the seeds with his fingers as though he were telling me that it was not necessary to blow them—there was an easier way!*
>
> *On another occasion I showed him the little rabbit that had just been born at the pony club. He looked at the baby and its mother for a long time and then repeated after me: "Baby and mother." The next day, I introduced him to the latest foals born at the club, saying, "Look, Luigi, young ponies." He replied, "Babies." Then he called to a little girl about his age, saying, "Come and see the babies!"*

Luigi speaks better each day and includes proper phrases in what he says. He is establishing relations with other people. What progress for just a year! His parents did not hesitate in moving house for the sake of their boy, in order to be closer to my pony club. He is turning into a great little rider, and his participation is for me an enormous reward.

The parents of an autistic child are often fully aware of what their child is going through but they can also be in a partial state of denial.

As Nicolas de Lahaye says, "Just imagine what it is like to be the parent of a child who pays no attention to you and does not even seem aware that he is a human being. He is unable to share thoughts or emotions and creates a space between you that no one can cross."

I become very involved with and sympathetic toward parents and caregivers of autistic children. They have heart-rending experiences all the time, but once they develop confidence in me, I can share their fears, their worries and their moments of progress with them. We support each other through the difficult times; we bring hope to each other; and we look to the future together.

I have so much respect for these parents and caregivers and what they have gone through. Often they have consulted specialists who have no more idea than they themselves in regards to how autism came about and how to cope with it. Occasionally they have acknowledged that there is something wrong but reject what they notice, perhaps in the hope that it will evaporate. At the pony club they are in a position to watch their child and his progress, to keep the distance they need to take a balanced view of what has happened to them all, without any sense of danger either to him or to themselves.

These moments are a revelation, partly because autistic children are such naturally good horsemen. Their improved posture will often come as a surprise, and it may be the first time they have seen their child excelling at an activity. Moreover they actually witness the course of his progress. Together with me we may hear his first words, and they see him building a relationship with the pony and with me. Soon parents feel that a real relationship between them and their child is for the first time a possibility, something they may have long ago despaired of ever seeing. We rejoice together in his progress and it gives us all new courage.

The parents themselves will often feel as though they have been allowed a fresh start, almost as though it were they who were in the saddle as well, as their child. What they learn at the club soon spills over into home life. The child becomes aware of spaces at home, just as he has acknowledged those at the club. He names things once he learns to speak; he looks up and down and from side to side; he notices and names colors and smells, fruits and vegetables, the furniture at home; he establishes markers and boundaries just as he does at the club.

No longer do the challenges of autism form a barrier to dialogue. The child has been returned to the parents as they have to their own life, though their role in the transformation becomes ever more evident and time-consuming. They often tell me about the problems they have experienced before they came to the club. Steven's history is a case in point.

Steven

When Steven came home from the hospital where he was born, he cried whenever he was separated from his parents. He literally needed to have them near him at every waking moment. When he reached nine months old, Steven could not be separated from his stroller. Whenever his parents took him out in order to encourage some activity, he screamed.

In the case of such a hypersensitive child, Nicolas de Lahaye interprets this as the baby's "emotional skin" and the mother's being one and the same thing: when the parent leaves him it is as though he is suddenly denuded, bereft of his psychic body envelope. He is crying out for his own "skin"—his own envelope. Nicolas de Lahaye interprets the stroller as also being part of the child's skin, especially where his seat and his back were in contact with it.

At the age of sixteen months, Steven would put up with being pushed to the park by his mother, but it still gave him no sense of autonomy: the stroller and his mother were all part of the same body envelope. It was no different at twenty months when he began to walk: stroller, mother, and the park were inexorably linked together: without his mother he could not abide being in the park, even though he was fine when she was present.

When Steven reached two, he turned in on himself completely. His mother had been asking for help since Steven was nine months old, and the doctor had said the child had problems with his sight and hearing. They sent Steven to a specialist who operated on his ears, inserting draining tubes. His mother told me that this operation aggravated his condition, and thereafter, Steven appeared to be even more withdrawn. I regret to say that it was the doctor who was deaf to the real situation, not the child, and this was only the beginning of a series of exams given by psychologists and neurologists, as well as blood tests, eye tests, scans, and a lumbar puncture. These tests revealed nothing, and it was only after Steven had had to endure all this misery that the penny dropped: he was diagnosed as autistic.

The doctor in charge of the case recommended that an educational expert, specializing in these problems, should come to the house for one hour each week. By this time Steven was three-and-a-half and his mother decided that he was so agitated by these visits that she asked for them to be stopped.

At this juncture, Steven's mother contacted me. In fact, the family lived only a few miles away and Steven's grandmother had been my own children's nurse, and it was she who approached me. Her daughter-in-law was at the end of her tether: the doctors just told her that Steven was still too young to be sent to a specialized school.

Nearly four years have now elapsed and Steven is a very different little boy. I have built a close and warm relationship with Stephanie, his mother, and she trusts me completely. Together we have watched Steven scaling the stairs of his renewal. She has told me all kinds of details about their life and the problems they endured before coming to the pony club, not only with Steven, but with the medical profession. It has been so gratifying to see this child put himself together and form a good relationship with his mother.

In desperation parents sometimes cut themselves off from friends and outside contact

As anyone who has an autistic child knows, life is an ordeal. Some parents do their best to hide their child's symptoms from the outside world and do this, usually, by cutting themselves and their child off from any contact. I am very much against any behavior of this sort. It is essential for the child to engage in leisure activity with other children as they do at my pony club, where their parents also make friends with other parents. Friendship and support are what they all desperately need.

You have seen throughout this book the value I place on the role of the parents, and many of them have made individual contributions to the book. Take Ingrid Laulhe, whose daughter has been riding with me since she was only ten months old. Ingrid works in therapeutic riding herself. She wrote, "What do young children, and in particular, children with physical and mental challenges, need? They need to learn about themselves, to feel secure enough to explore on their own, accept challenges, experience different sensations, and to feel emotion—all these fill out their lives.

"What role does the pony have in all this? Firstly, it carries them, it resonates, it invites all sorts of muscles, especially those concerned with balance, to start working. It moves, sometimes taking the rider by surprise; it stops, occasionally without being asked to. It is warm; it feels strong. The dust it kicks up can sting the eyes, and occasionally, it trembles. Now and then it can make the rider a little nervous, and it can make him feel proud of himself. It can annoy him or calm him; it can make him want to sing and sometimes to shed a tear. It can knock into things and make the rider watch out where he is going; it makes him aware that there are always new circumstances so he has to learn to watch out and be prepared for the unexpected. Finally, it unconsciously rectifies imbalances in the body and makes the rider feel better because of being better balanced."

Lucy and Timothy

In September 2008, a girl called Lucy came to me. She was twelve years old and in a sad state: even in the saddle she was so rigid with fear that her legs stuck out at the front to the extent that it hurt, and she grasped the saddle with both hands. It took quite a few sessions before she adapted to the rhythm of the pony and became aware that she could trust it, arrange the position of her body, and relax her legs. Finally she was able to let go of the saddle, and I could see that her chest was moving in time with the pony's motion and no doubt much more comfortable than when everything was jiggling up and down uncontrollably.

Another autistic boy of thirteen, Timothy, soon became so proud of his skills he entertained himself by turning around in the saddle. A month later, he was holding the reins correctly and supporting himself on the stirrups at the trot.

It is astonishing how patient and understanding the ponies are. As you can imagine some of these children are very clumsy when they ride for the first time. Others are so curious that they pry open the pony's mouth, speak into its ears, and sniff it in various places.

Gradually the children learn that they can exert control over their pony, and no doubt, this gives them the idea of "otherness," but the control they have only goes so far. They have to respect the pony and the amount of control they can exert is dependent on the pony's cooperation.

At the same time they see that the pony responds to language just as they do, but theirs is richer. They also understand that they can be a little afraid of the pony and similarly the pony is a little afraid of them. It shies and complains if they are rough or unkind: they have to learn to treat it as they want the pony to treat them.

The pony holds them safely on its saddle; it rocks them comfortingly; it carries them along faster than they could move on their own legs; and it makes them feel like a little centaur. Their head is higher than their parents,' and this gives them a new feeling of independence and power; they can actually move outside the area where they can be seen by their parents, where they no longer have to think about whether the parents are approving of what they do.

However, all this takes place in total security. They gradually become aware that all these great sensations are only given to them if they treat the pony well and respect it properly. They have to learn about coopera-tion, give and take, and caring for an animal; the pony cannot groom itself so they have to do something essential for the pony if the animal is to remain in good condition with a lovely glossy coat; trying to be a "dictator" without giving anything in return does not work.

All this has been about the effects on the child of his relationship with the pony, but there is also an important effect on his parents. Their child is suddenly absent from their sphere of influence. Possibly for the first time, they do not know what is happening to him, and they have no direct responsibility for his safety. He is experimenting with the new sensation of being on his own without his parents, and they are suddenly experienc-ing the same sensation. For the child this is part of growing up; for the parents it is a necessary step in their own evolution vis-à-vis their child.

Part Two

My Journal

"Claudine's joie de vivre is something that everyone who meets her wants to be part of. The confidence and magnetism that she radiates persuades parents and those with autistim that she is someone to trust and confide in, whether the information is flattering to themselves or the reverse, because they know that she will not think any differently about them. She exudes warmth and confidence so that parents who perhaps had given up hope feel prepared to try again and place their trust in her.

"All that can be said of the autistic children is that they are literally transported into a new experience where pony and person are conflated into an agreeable sensation that allows them to peer out of their self-protective 'prison' and then head for the open ground. From the first moment it is a positive feeling for them: it matters not whether the postural and other therapeutic effects of contact with a moving pony or Claudine's magnetic personality are the most important factors. Autistic children and parents rebuild their life: they take due account of their problems but also their blessings creating viable lives."

—Nicolas de Lahaye

Journal Introduction

This part of the book takes the form of an inventory. Every child has a unique character and has therefore to be treated to some degree differently, even if the principles are the same. When the wrong approach is used it can have a negative effect; if it seems aggressive, it will only drive the child farther back into his protective "prison" and make impossible any feeling of confidence he might have—and indeed must have—in order to make progress.

I have arranged this journal according to the development of my knowledge and experience over a number of years with, in particular, three young autistic children: Lucien, Steven, and Victor, who I have already introduced you to in Part One of this book. When they came to me at the request of their parents, Lucien was two-and-a-half years old, Steven three-and-a-half, and Victor, ten. The period of therapeutic riding has been in Lucien's case five years, three-and-a-half for Steven, and only six months for Victor. During this period there have, of course, also been other children under my care who have enriched my understanding.

The history of these children recounted as the events occurred will make some of the information in the first part of the book seem redundant or repetitious, but I wanted to give a sense of the time scale. There has been progress in all three cases but also long periods in which progress seemed to be coming slowly, stagnating, or even retreating. You will, perhaps, be conscious of my own periods of doubt and reflection, but in the end I trust it will encourage all readers to hold on to hope during the difficult periods, for you will see children developing contact with their body, their feelings, their emotions—and with other people.

Lucien

At two-and-a-half-years old, Lucien arrived with his brother for a riding session along with six other kids, and at that point I had not been told that Lucien was autistic.

We were right in the middle of the holiday period, and I had arranged two groups to alternate with each other. In the first group the children were to learn about grooming their pony and preparing it for a ride— brushing its coat and inspecting hooves in case there was anything that needed attention. The second group started as soon as the first group had dismounted.

My attention was particularly drawn to Lucien, a frail little boy with what I would call an absent air about him. He looked no more than two years old so I gave him Tarquin, the most senior and experienced of all my ponies, whose task is always to carry the youngest of the children. When all the children were saddled up I started them walking calmly around the space, encouraging them to relax and enjoy themselves, so that I could study each one and get some idea about their ability. Lucien appeared to like the rhythmic movement like all the rest.

Then I asked for a halt and immediately Lucien began to scream, exactly in the manner of an eighteen-month-old who commonly dislikes it when the movement ceases. He was clearly unhappy with this procedure: the movement only had to stop and he shrieked. His mother came to the rescue, took him in her arms and left the ring. I suggested they return in a couple of days. I admit I was a little thrown by the child's piercing shriek and seeing his face contorted with pain like a baby. I understood that, in fact, here was a "baby" that could not tolerate cessation of movement. But I continued calmly with the rest of the children.

When I next saw Lucien's mother she came without him, explaining that it was the same with the stroller: he could not bear it when the movement stopped, and yes, he was autistic. After the last session he had messed himself really badly, something he didn't usually do. I recalled that when I first met Lucien, he had watched a pony defecating and said, "Poop."

When his mother said they were returning for another session, Lucien repeated the word "Poop" before saying "No!" I thought it a good idea to reassure his mother in that at least he had said two words correctly, and that it was no bad thing to have evacuated and shown disagreement with a proposal. We had to wait for a propitious moment to try again.

July 2003

Lucien came back a few months later accompanied by his brother and his grandparents who conveniently lived in the village close to the pony club and regularly took the children during the holidays. He and his brother were both enrolled for a riding session, and subsequently they brought Lucien every two days throughout the first half of July. When they arrived, Lucien's grandmother had pushed him all the way through the woods in the stroller and explained to me that he loved it and was very reluctant to leave it.

Like all autistic children, when faced with an unfamiliar environment, Lucien examined the periphery of the arena before looking at anything close by. He went into the part where the ponies are stabled as if to check on everything, and I noticed that his gaze fixed on a Shetland that was already saddled up. Without saying a word I popped on his riding helmet, took the halter of the Shetland and led him into the riding area. I skipped the usual step of getting the child to groom the pony and caress it before riding because I sensed Lucien would not at this stage like the direct contact with the pony's warm hide; better to get him straight into the saddle, which I achieved with a feeling of relief.

Sensing also that Lucien would need individual attention, I had set aside a one-on-one session so that I could concentrate all my faculties in observing him and being guided by him. It was in my estimation already an achievement to have got him into the saddle without a serious problem, and I felt we had made the first step toward a relationship.

I set off around the arena holding the pony and only taking quick glances at him so that he would feel no pressure from me. I had no idea at that moment how things were going to turn out: I just concentrated on being the receptacle for his anxieties. I already felt strangely close to him and began to have an idea of his skills, though I was not trying to judge him or impose some sort of model behavior.

When I got home I took some notes and thought about what I had experienced. I considered that when Lucien cried out, it represented an appeal to another person, in this case, me. Autistic children have their own ways of communicating and of declaring their feelings of anxiety: it is one way of being heard by the outside world. From that day on I took these cries to be an appeal for help, just as it is with babies.

A family that has been bringing its children to the club regularly arrived with their latest, a girl, only nine months old. The mother told me that she was completely exhausted because the child cried so much during the night she could never get enough sleep.

I suggested trying her on a pony; the mother agreed, so with her holding the baby, we put her on the saddle and set off at a walk. I noticed that her little body followed the movement of the pony admirably, but then, by chance, she met my eyes and burst into tears. At the second session, her father held her, and I was able to exchange the occasional eye contact with her without her crying. At the third session she smiled at me and allowed me to hold her on the saddle. Since then the mother has been left in peace.

My autistic pupils' parents are so pleased with my work, attributing my skill to the lessons I have learned in the process of teaching babies to ride, that I derive tremendous comfort and a great feeling of reward. My horses also give me this feeling especially when I am a bit overwhelmed with all the emotion and heartache involved. When I feel the work is getting me down I go for a ride in the woods and allow the horse to absorb my anxieties and tiredness, just as he does with the children.

There are great demands placed on the teachers of autistic children. We have to be totally committed, have a sensitive nature, and have strong motherly instincts. Also, since an autistic child starts by refusing any outside influence, a teacher has to have the gift of being able to delve deeply into the child's psyche in order to reach those primitive, early moments when his life took the wrong turn. I feel I am on a quest to discover ancient markers that are the foundation stones of personality. I have to return to the point at which the "blockage" occurred, and it is no easy matter to set out from a place that is so deep inside.

My sessions with autistic kids always begin with a calming walk: it was the same with Lucien. I walked quietly alongside him without meeting his eye, while he slowly built up his confidence. Some children are really upset if you make eye contact and they start to scream, so I avoid it if at all possible. For this session I had arranged posts in a line at three-yard intervals so that Lucien could grab a ring I had placed around one of them and transfer it to another and vice-versa. This exercise also gets across a sense of time passing; the time it takes to transfer a ring from one post to another.

At first Lucien grabbed a ring and held on to it. I took one and placed it on another post; when I had repeated this several times, Lucien imitated me. We started again and repeated the game a dozen times, while always extending the time gap between each action.

Repetition is an essential part of teaching autistic children: they have to repeat something until they are quite secure. The session lasted a full quarter hour before Lucien was happy to stop, and I had another two sessions with him alone before including him with other children. In the group sessions the kids all circulate around the arena, and Lucien was soon imitating the others. I have noticed that being in a group often has a good effect, and there is even something special about the act of moving around a space in a circular and repeated way. Denys Ribas reckons the children emerge from this exercise a fraction stronger, as if the circular, repeating motion becomes a spiral of progress.

The arena where I keep all the play objects, including the so-called "autistic objects," also makes a huge contribution in that handling the objects opens lines of communication between the teachers and the children, as well as between the children themselves. But the pony is undoubtedly the star, the key factor in their progress.

One day I was visited by some caregivers from a group called, La Farandole, from Nogent-le-Retrou, France. They brought with them two groups of children between eighteen months and two years old. The first group consisted of six children whom I had the time to talk with and observe before we mounted them on the six ponies that were prepared for them. Four of them were completely at ease, but the other two were in tears at first, although soon calmed by the motion of the ponies.

The second group consisted of a dozen children whom I divided into two groups before putting them on the ponies. This time there were no tears and all the children left with a smile. Thinking about what I had done that was different with the first and second group, I decided that I had been the cause of the tears because I looked the children in the eye. I learned my lesson. When I discussed the event with Nicolas de Lahaye he observed that their reaction was fear of a direct look, and indirectly, fear of our passionate interest in their well-being.

Part of the reason why the ponies have such a remarkable effect is that the child, once in the saddle, does not feel alone. Not only is he rocked and "contained" by the pony, he is thrown into a relationship that I am also part of, due to my own relationship with the pony. Normally an autistic child has great difficulty in reciprocating any form of communication, but has little difficulty with the pony, so with patience and understanding, I can establish a three-cornered relationship with the two of them. The children seem to be aware of my closeness to the ponies and think of me as some sort of extension of the animal—they call me "Madame Pony"!

April 2004

During the period from July 2003 to April 2004, Lucien did not come to stay with his grandparents for vacation, but I couldn't get him out of my head, and when we met again, we clicked as if I had seen him the day before.

During the course of the first session, Lucien suddenly jumped off the pony and climbed into a large plastic container where he was hidden from view. I had come across this pattern of behavior with other autistic children: suddenly dismounting when they are apparently quite content and when there is no obvious reason for it. In Lucien's case there was also the fact that he disappeared into a solid structure, so I thought maybe it was something to do with the permanence of the container that appealed to him.

I waited quietly until he emerged and caught sight of me. He dived back into the container and could no longer see me. He appeared to be surprised by this phenomenon so I made a game of it. I burst out laughing and exactly in the manner of little babies, he laughed too. We repeated the game several times, and he could understand that I would still be there even though he could not see me. Following on this experience, I introduced the game of hide and seek as one of the tools I work with.

April 2004 to June 2005

During this period Lucien came to stay with his grandparents in all the school holidays. Working with him, I developed the use of gestures to help the children imitate what was happening. I had already used this technique with babies to great effect, so it was easy to develop it further with the autistic kids who would imitate my arm movements and then repeat them with the other children in the group. The exercises involved stretching in all directions while in the saddle: forward, backward and to either side, grasping objects and moving them—in the case of the rings— to another place.

I often debated with myself whether it was a good idea to let the children manipulate the balls and rings in a typically autistic, repetitive way, but Nicolas de Lahaye reassured me. I decided not to pay any attention when a child started turning an object over repeatedly or even wanted to keep it at the end of the session, though in principle the children were not allowed to take objects home. I understood that when this happened, the child suddenly felt the need to retreat into his self-protective world, and I should not prevent it.

During this period Lucien made great progress both linguistically and in his ability to participate in the games and integrate with the other kids. He could take objects, just like the others, and move them from one place to another. More important, we could hold what could almost be called conversations, as long as I adapted my language to his limitations and took account of his perceptions.

I try to make a logical progression in the kind of games we play, first emphasizing the purely visual aspects—for instance the appearance and disappearance of an object. Then I introduce games that favor the idea of relationship—for instance, I make a point of saying, "For you," when I hand them an object, and, "For me," when they return it. I might also say, "I give it to you," and "You give it to me." This is important because often autistic children have no concept, at first, of "you" and "me."

I soon became adept at picking up the slightest hint of emotion, whether one of suffering or joy. I have to notice where they are looking, what sounds they are registering, and the bodily sensations they become aware of. In the saddle, there is contact with the saddle, the pony itself, and various parts of the child's body. This contact changes and develops with movement, and of course there are further changes as the pony goes through different paces. Then, there is the discovery that they can influence the pace and the position of the pony. I try to make the kids aware of these changes and of what is going on in their body. When describing any interaction with the pony, I make sure to use the same gestures, the same words and phrases and in the same order: it must all be logical and concrete so that it does not induce muddle in their mind. You could say that it is not dissimilar from the way in which horses are trained: instructions, whether by body movement, weight distribution, activity with the hands or legs, or indeed by voice, must each time be repeated in a similar way and clearly in order not to muddle the horse and frighten him.

As I have said, I use gestures a lot in order to introduce new movements and games. I do not expect ever to have immediate results. I know I must repeat many times but not so often that the child becomes bored and retreats into his shell. If I see any sign of boredom, then I switch to another game. All this I have learned from working with babies. The techniques I use with the autistic children are not exactly the same but owe a lot to them. Handling the reins is a particularly hard lesson to get across. Autistic children take a long time to understand the connection between the pony's mouth, the reins, and their hands. If it is too difficult at an early stage, then I tie the reins on the neck.

It must be obvious to anyone that learning to ride is not just an intellectual process, and this is indeed its great merit. Every new experience—for instance, turning, speeding up, slowing down, changing pace, jumping over an obstacle, or coming to a halt—creates a new combination of physical sensations that may come about because the instructor has demonstrated or described a new movement, or simply by experiment. These new sensations have to be understood by the body, assimilated by the limbs, as well as being understood by the brain and put into the memory.

November 2005

I returned to the pony club with a group of children to find Lucien waiting for me, as always, in the same place. He then entered the club with me where we often worked with his favorite "objects" he used for support. I was trying at this stage to extend the range of objects that he would touch or play with. He refused to touch anything with a soft surface like his pony or a large deflated balloon. In fact, the first time he put his hand out to feel the balloon he withdrew it as if he had been burned. He only liked hard objects.

We would go up to one of his objects, pick it up, turn it around, manipulate it, and finally throw it onto the ground. After this we might play some games in which I would name the objects and the actions. I remember there was one game that he disliked, consisting of filling and emptying a container. He carried it out only once for me, and with considerable aplomb, but then there were no repeats. I had the impression that he did it correctly in order to please me but that was that.

April 2006

Lucien was given to babbling a lot. I would then seize on a word and use it in a short phrase that made sense of it. In this way we began to build up his language ability and soon we could hold conversations.

July 2006

Lucien began to show more and more curiosity during our excursions in the woods. I took the opportunity to put names to all the plants and objects that caught his attention. I also guided him over and around as many natural obstacles and uphill and downhill tracks as I could find. The woods used to be divided into different parcels of land and the ancient demarcations are still there in places. I delighted in using these obstacles to extend the range of Lucien's bodily and mental experiences. I could see that he was feeling his body in all sorts of new ways; sometimes he would swivel around to look behind him or at other riders in the vicinity. All the time he was experiencing new positions of his body and weight as the pony negotiated the uneven terrain, learning at the same time what was required in order to keep his balance. This was particularly important for Lucien since on level ground he tended to look straight ahead.

August 2006

Lucien rode up such a steep rise that the pony gave a big shove with its hindquarters at the same time as it raised its head, resulting in Lucien hitting his own head on the pony's neck. I could see that it was very much a case of encountering the "other" and for a few seconds, he lost his usual feeling of being in balance.

November 2006

Lucien was cementing his relationships—not only with me but with the other children, too.

February 2007

Lucien was telling me about dinosaurs and his Action Man that he took out of his bag to show me. He brandished the figure in a simulation of an attack mode. Although, or perhaps because the Action Man seemed to be very important to him, he handed it to me for safekeeping during the session. This demonstrated a newfound confidence in me that I treasured, at the same time as I realized how fragile it was. I am constantly on the lookout for any sign that I might be in some way putting at risk the progress we have made together, and I feel more and more that I am taking my lead from Lucien about the steps he needs or is prepared to take in order to enter our world.

March 2007

Lucien was now building connections in space and time between the riding sessions and his outside life. He often went to a clinic's daycare, and he told the people there about coming to me during vacation. The fact that he knows he has to wait for it to begin helps to establish the idea of events in his life arriving from outside him. He is now able to speak about something or someone who is not present—me, for example.

It was fascinating to witness the progression in Lucien's improvement. To see how his body reacted to and resonated with that of the pony at each of the different paces, and to know that these were helping to feed his growing awareness not only of time and space, but how time was structured by them, just as when he moved objects from one position to another.

April 2007

Lucien's language skills had by now made great progress. He was constructing entire sentences and able to use the "I" as well as express his fears in words. I remember the occasion when he grabbed one of the toy foam lances, and I took the opportunity to suggest we go and attack some of the monsters, dragons, and dinosaurs that seemed to haunt his life. I said to him, "Monsters, dragons, and dinosaurs are so frightened of ponies that we probably will not see any." And, of course, we didn't, but the act of hunting for them helped to allay his fears merely because we had gone on an expedition without encountering them: no doubt confidence in the pony, and by extension, his own prowess increased.

Then there was the case of Victor, another child, at this time ten years old, who was able to express his fears when he was on horseback. He had been thrown out of his therapy groups because he became violent and was considered a danger to others. It was a kind of challenge for me to see if I could make any breakthroughs with this child who had been rejected by the standard therapy groups.

He began by coming to the pony club every Tuesday morning. At first, he appeared terrified of the horses' mouth and perhaps their eyes.

When young children express such fears I usually calm them by telling them about how gentle these animals are and that they could soon overcome any fear by getting to know them and watching them. In Victor's case, as soon as we put him in a saddle and set off, the sight of his horse's mouth and eyes no longer made him afraid.

He soon came to more sessions each week; like Lucien, his language was full of references to monsters and crocodiles. At the end of one session he was reluctant to leave the club, and I saw that he was shouting, "Nasty boy!" in an aggressive manner. The two caregivers in charge of him came running up in order to get him under control but without thinking of any possible danger, I went up to him and said, "No, Victor, you are a gentle young man and also a great horseman." Since that day I have been able to put my hands on him occasionally. At other times he simply cries out, "Don't touch me!"

Lucien and Victor were both the same in that neither could assume a fantasy role in order to grapple with their fears. If I suggested to Lucien that he might be a knight in shining armor, he replied, "I am Lucien." Likewise, his fears could not be transformed into the stuff of myth or make-believe. They were real to him. He was always picking up one of the sponge batons and attacking the other riders with a shout of "Yaaa!" I tried to deflect these attacks by telling him he was a knight and had to find other knights to attack, but he became so obsessively involved in this game that I had to hide the batons from him.

Summer Vacation 2007

Even though the day finally arrived when Lucien made the leap of imagi-nation needed to understand that letters make up a word and the word actually stands for something (see more of this story on p. 97), I took care not to have any expectations for the next time we met. Imposing my expec-tations would have been a source of anxiety he was not ready for.

It is the same for very young children to whom I owe so much of what I have learned: I must leave them time to absorb newly acquired concepts at their own speed and in their own way. Working with them made me rely enormously on my intuition, and I use this faculty all the time with the autistic children in order to establish a good relationship with them.

I have learned the hard way that anxiety weighs heavily on autistic children, and one must not aggravate these fears by inappropriate behav-ior or use of words. For instance, I soon noticed that when a parent says, "Don't be frightened," it has the opposite effect. When I am putting a child onto the saddle for the first time I always tell the parents to say nothing but to help me lift the child on board and rely on the pony to take over and achieve the calming effect that the parent so desires. Of course there are occasions when I have to act on the spur of the moment, but I feel so close and at ease now with my autistic charges that I feel confident of doing the right thing in emergencies. Their security and well-being is my aim, and at the pony club they can explore, feel, hear, and touch with immunity and in total security.

March 2008

Months after Lucien first noticed the big letters in the dressage arena, he pointed out the letters written on his pony's saddle that made out its name. Like many of the other children, the pony's name was the first step in understanding the symbolical significance of lettering. By now he was speaking articulately and even pointing out, with a degree of humor, any clumsiness on my part.

One of his favorite occupations was playing with the hard plastic toys that either represented farm animals or jungle creatures. He also had an impressive collection of figures in different outfits. He was very particular about what games he played. He continued to carry one of the little soft swords in his pocket to protect himself. He had now been admitted half-time to a class in which children with various challenges are integrated with "normal" children, and for the other half he still went to daycare.

July 2009

I hadn't seen Lucien for a whole year when he came back on a visit accompanied by his father. As soon as he caught sight of me he ran up and threw himself into my arms. We had planned for him to come for a riding session the next day, but he was so eager to start that I took him on the spot. He asked for Figaro, his favorite pony, and he was from the first moment completely at home in the saddle: he had forgotten nothing. Strangely, he still carried the little toy sword in his pocket.

As we set off on our excursion to the woods I told him I was taking him to see my magic tree. It's a stunning tree with its trunk all covered in creeper, but Lucien did not find it was magical. "It can't be magic," he said, "there are no goblins." "How are we going to find some?" I asked. "We'll buy a book with goblins in it; we'll count one, two, three, and then pounce on them," he said. "That's a grand idea!" I replied.

Lucien was now speaking excellently. While he was on holiday with his grandparents, he came occasionally to ride with me and I noticed that toward the end of the holiday, he no longer carried the sword. When I asked him about it, he simply said that he no longer needed it.

When he left, I said to him, "I'm going to miss you, Lucien," to which he replied, "You are going to call me!"

His grandparents gave me the home telephone number, and I did not forget to call him.

Steven

April 2003

On the recommendation of her mother-in-law, who happened to have been my own children's nanny, Stephanie came to me with Steven, her two-and-a-half-year-old son. He had been diagnosed with autism only six months previously. He had already caught sight of me a number of times when I went to collect my own children, so I was not a complete stranger to him. As soon as he arrived he looked at me, and then began to caress, with very rapid strokes, the pony I indicated was the one I had chosen for him. I helped him into the saddle and off we set for the woods.

At that point, Steven discovered the babies' sandpit, and at the end of each ride, he sat in it, snatching the odd furtive glance at the other children rather in the manner of a frightened animal, and ceaselessly running the sand through his fingers. At the end of the first year he began to fill and empty plastic vessels in the sandpit. Nicolas de Lahaye says that this behavior, which is common enough with autistic children under the age of seven, indicates that the child is racked by the fear of meltdown, or of leaking away like water from a container. Filling a vessel with sand helps him to feel contained, and this action should not be likened to a child without autism playing in a similar way.

After they reach the age of seven, I have noticed that autistic children no longer make for the sandpit; they dump themselves in a corner and resort to repetitive stereotypical movements like rocking. Slightly older children can also become hyperactive.

June 2005

By this time I was taking Steven once or twice a week. I built a close relationship with his mother, Stephanie, who was distraught by her son's strange comportment. When she had approached her doctor and her family for help she found only incomprehension. Such is the air of misunderstanding that frequently surrounds autism. Steven was noticeably calmer when in the saddle, and his body motion accompanied that of the pony in a remarkably relaxed and light manner. He looked great! That the pony also "contained" him was all too evident because when he was not in the saddle, he took to his heels.

Fortunately, he could only escape within the confines of the arena, the saddling enclosure, and the sand pit; he seemed quite happy circling these areas and exploring them. I encouraged him to look about in front, behind, up, and down, and I hoped that this increasing awareness of his surroundings would give him an understanding of space and subsequently, of other things and other people.

August 2005

Three months elapsed before I integrated Steven into a group session with other children. Even then, I had to pay more attention to him than to the others, so that one day a little girl in the class complained to me that I always paid more attention to him than to anyone else. I explained to her that Steven needed her help as well in order to grow up. I told her that I had not forgotten her but that she was so grown up herself, and rode so well, that she needed less help than Steven. From that day she became a real friend to Steven, probably the first he had ever had, and I am very grateful to her for that.

September 2005

By now Steven was imitating the others in his group, moving objects from one position to another, for instance, when he transferred a ring from the top of a vertical post to a horizontal one down low.

Occasionally, it was all too much for him and then he retreated into his shell: I did not stop him and reckoned the fact that he reacted to what he considered too great a pressure showed that he recognized the existence of others and situations outside himself.

October 2005

Steven was intrigued by horse droppings, while at the same time he was taking a class at the local clinic designed to teach him about cleanliness. Like most children, whether autistic or not, Steven was a little frightened about the substances that come out of the body and watching the ponies urinate and defecate was essentially reassuring. When he began with me, he was still wearing diapers; this is not unusual at his age, autistic or not.

At this juncture Steven was particularly enjoying the games involving balls and balloons, even if some of them were treated as "autistic objects" and played with in a repetitive manner.

The work by André Bullinger on the development of sensory/motor ability were a particular help to me in achieving good posture in my young riders and in teaching them to use their arms. He also talks about the points of support where the seat is on the saddle and the role these points play in joining the two halves of the body.

Babies (under eighteen months) have a good seat in the saddle: it has the effect of pushing forward the base of the spine a little. This enables babies to sit up, and you can see their faces lighting up with the increased confidence it affords them, allowing them also to look about them and take in what is going on.

It was Catherine Dolto who alerted me to the advantages of the Western saddle. It is a great help in producing a really good position of the spine that, in turn, automatically establishes a better position of the head in relation to the spine. I now use them on all my ponies, and it is noticeable how the autistic children are soon able to look about them and begin to explore their surroundings with their eyes.

Steven was a good example of the benefits offered by using a Western saddle: during the session I could see him "uncurling" his spine. Once his spine was erect, the head followed, and soon he was focusing his eyes and looking about at different objects or people. His body's movements coordinated with those of the pony most impressively.

November 2005

Steven was becoming more and more at ease with his body and carrying out experiments that appeared to be testing the possibilities of movement. He would lean far over to the side or backward but always stop just in time to avoid losing his balance, all the while adjusting to the pony's movement. The feelings these exercises produced provoked a real dialog between his physical and emotional makeup. I could see him discovering new possibilities as he waved his arms about and tried out new positions with his torso.

A young child pieces together a world out of the things he touches, smells, and hears. A horse sends him a continuous stream of varying sensations as long as he is in the saddle. His body has to follow the horse's rhythm, and these sensations that he receives from the outside help him to construct what we call the psychic body envelope (see p. 12). From there it is a step to understanding the difference between "outside" and "inside" the envelope. The child feels his body moving with the pony, but then his senses become aware of smell, sight, and touch. An autistic child needs the help from the pony to accept the experience of touching and subsequently of being touched: for the first time he sees that touching can be a pleasurable experience in both directions.

When he started, Steven was insensitive to pain. I have seen him being pricked in several places by a thorn bush without apparently feeling anything. Nowadays, a year later, he is aware of this sort of experience.

February 2006

When I asked Steven to reach up and touch the big balloon, he had to raise his hand and then his arm to a vertical position. At that point, he could no longer see his hand but he still went ahead with the action of touching the balloon. Thus he became aware that, even though he could no longer see his hand, it nevertheless continued to exist, and he was able to carry out a planned action while it was out of sight.

In order to extend the lessons learned by this game I arranged for a pulley to be installed that could raise and lower the big balloon and this obligated Steven to reach farther and farther into the space above him. When I play this game I begin with a yellow balloon because yellow is usually the color the young children in my program favor. Later, I replace the yellow balloon with blue for the boys and pink for the girls. Autistic children are often attracted to the color red but Steven still prefers blue, which makes me realize that you cannot make hard-and-fast rules about these preferences: each child is unique.

Playing with balloons was the means of introducing Steven to all sorts of other games, and from then on, I was able to introduce variations or new games at all the sessions. At the next session I taught Steven, along with some other kids, to empty and fill baskets containing balls and to move them from one place to another. I got the message across to him by making the gestures required for transferring the balls a number of times while he accompanied me on his pony. When he imitated me I gave him a cheer, and then he continued to do it by himself while also watching and imitating the other riders in the group. He had already got the idea of imitation from his games in the sandpit where he had learned to fill and empty a bucket with sand.

Later, Steven succeeded in placing cones on the top of posts of different lengths. This exercise was carried out while the pony was moving and therefore the objects appeared and disappeared as he circulated. I withdrew a little so he could concentrate on what he was doing and not feel that I was involved in some way with what was happening. I wanted him to understand that the experience was as a result of his interaction with an object and nothing to do with my presence.

March 2006

Steven, while playing in the sandpit, threw down the balls he was turning around in his hands, and this action gave him the understanding of depth, and therefore, that the world is not one-dimensional. In the saddle he no longer needed me there while he transferred play balls from one basket to another. What he could see with his eyes was enough to dictate his action.

The rules of the game were that the balls had not only to be removed from one basket but placed in a net that held them. At first, Steven would remove the balls and throw them on the ground. He was indeed discovering the concept of depth so I did not correct him but simply went through the correct action myself. I could see that he was taking it all in even though he did nothing at the time. Later on, however, when the session was over, he returned to the arena and lifted the balls that he had thrown onto the ground into the appropriate net. I reckon these games helped this boy to understand the concept of the spaces he inhabited, and his position in those spaces.

June 2006

We were in a clearing in the woods; the riders had dismounted to let their ponies graze when Steven got a thorn in his calf. He scratched the place that hurt and began to cry. His mother had already remarked that he was becoming more sensitive to any sensation involving his skin. The pony was playing an important role in teaching him about pleasant tactile sensations, and here was an unpleasant one. He soon learned to accept both: he had developed from not feeling lots of thorns in several places, to feeling only one.

August 2006

Steven pulled his riding cap over his eyes and then lifted it up again. Surprised by the effect he repeated this game several times. This caused me to laugh out loud and say, "Peekaboo!" when his eyes were uncovered. This game went on for months and I introduced a variation by hiding behind a pillar or a wall: I appeared and disappeared so that he understood about the permanence of an object—the fact that it still existed even though it could not for the moment be seen.

Little children adore the game of hide-and-seek. When he was four years old, Steven loved to hide and lie down in a plastic container in the play arena that was used to carry the toys and objects there. He would suddenly emerge, burst into laughter when he saw me, and go back again.

Three-year-old Luigi only started holding my gaze after nine months at the club. By that time we were exchanging real meaningful looks, and he would either smile or lower his cap in order to hide his eyes as though the intensity of this exchange were more than he could bear. Nicolas de Lahaye explained it as follows: it was a progression from two-dimensionality to three-dimensionality. A look is not just something on the surface: it has an inner meaning.

October 2006

Steven spoke his first words: they seemed to emerge from very far down and with difficulty. Now we could start to look at things together and name them. Steven took my hand in his as though it were an extension of his own to show me an ants' nest in a tree trunk. Genevieve Haag calls this development the moment when the child "recovers his first skin." I held his hand for a time and then withdrew it so that I could point independently at the nest and he could imitate me. I felt it was time that he began to appreciate the separateness of our bodies and that he could act independently.

Genevieve Haag has some interesting theories about the way in which an autistic child or adult has a tendency to attach himself—in a lateral sense—to another person. He wants to hold the other person's hand almost in the manner of a lover and seek his support. You have to allow this at first but gradually the autistic person has to be weaned away progressively so that he builds, and then becomes aware of and appreciates, his own vertical axis. As we have seen, the pony is a great aid to this process.

This is the third stage in which the autistic child starts by accepting the pony in a fearless relationship, sees me as an extension of the pony, and can then touch the various parts of my body as well as his own: arms, hands, and knees. He will often want to attach himself to me just as he attaches himself to the pony. He discovers his own body at the same time as he discovers more about the space around him.

My "baby riders" discover their own body piece by piece. Thanks to the process of riding, they see that the hands have to carry out various movements in order to persuade the pony to turn to either side, and to stop. They also discover that their legs are required to get moving, an action they find easier to grasp than the action of the hands, because it requires the understanding of the connection between the mouth of the pony and their hands through the reins. In the long run, riding moves every part of the body and opens a dialog between their body position and their emotions. The children see their body in movement and begin, therefore, to distinguish between their own motion and that of the horse.

At home, Steven's family helped to develop this understanding. Steven was able to name the different parts of his body, which not only gave him a greater understanding of his own body but the recognition of other people's limbs, as well.

February 2007

This was the occasion when Steven knocked over some posts and picked up the riding crop that I called "my magic wand," while fixing me with his gaze. After dismounting, he looked at me, clearly awaiting my reaction. I started by making a face and giving him a rather severe look with wide-stretched eyes. Then I said, "I'm angry with you, Steven," and pointed at the overturned posts. He immediately righted the posts and stood there waiting for my reaction. Since I was pleased, I smiled at him and told him so. He was perfectly well aware of his actions because he could say "Angry or happy?" to me.

This was an exploration of the world of emotions and feeling: he knew that when he was happy, I was too, and this double awareness gave him confidence in our relationship and helped him to continue the building process. He accepted the fact that I was upset or pleased with him, but in telling him, I hardly changed the tone of my voice. After all, I don't raise my voice with the ponies, and the children would not respect me if I did and might well run away from me. So I remained absolutely calm while I said to Steven, "Now Steven, put my magic wand back where it belongs." He did so without demur: it was a calm, clear request that made sense in the context and he had no problem in carrying it out.

At this stage Steven clearly understood and accepted that we were two different people. I was no longer an extension either of him or of the horse. He could also understand the difference between "inside" and "outside." Sensations arriving unbidden from the outside were no longer acts of aggression, even if they hurt a little physically. He had become aware of touch and sensations of pain. He was beginning to use his sense of smell, for instance when he sniffed the vegetables in my garden. For Genevieve Haag this fourth stage is distinguished by the disappearance of the stereotypical repetitive actions, the emergence of sexual rivalry that can on occasion be very strong, and finally the emergence of grammar in their speech.

March 2007

As far as his riding skills were concerned, I was now working on the trot, the canter, and the gallop. He still did not grasp the actions he would have to use in order to initiate these different paces by means of his hands, legs, and voice. Usually autistic children do understand fairly quickly the result of applying their legs in order to encourage forward motion, but he compensated by having a wonderful light and balanced seat "like an air cushion" said one of the instructors working with me.

On one occasion Steven was at full gallop and as usual was carried away with the thrill of it when he leaped off without losing his balance and in the most agile way. He rushed up to his mother, crying out, "Mom!" and they hugged each other. His mother later told me that this was the first time she had experienced such a fond hug.

June 2007

I had not seen Steven for some months because he had been unwell. As soon as he arrived at the pony club he named parts of his face while he pointed to them with his hand: eyes, mouth, nose, and so on. I did the same thing with mine as we looked into the mirror we were standing next to. When I had last seen him we often played the game of touching various parts of our own and each other's face while naming them, and it was this that he wanted to do immediately—doubtless in order to feel at ease.

August 2007

During the summer vacation Steven did not come to the club, but I was told he began to show signs of agitation. He sat by the window waiting for the taxi that, during the school term, came to fetch him and bring him to the club. When none of the cars that passed turned out to be the taxi, he cried and even screamed, so his mother phoned me and asked if she could bring him over. I agreed, and after a couple of daily sessions, the agitation disappeared; he still sat by the window watching the cars go by but no longer cried when they failed to stop.

Before Stephanie goes shopping she usually brings Steven to the pony club for a session to calm him down. He is rather fearful of crowds and is less likely to cause trouble if he has been for a ride. The contact with the pony helps him to get himself together and be emotionally calm. Didier Houzel talks about the intolerable emotional strain that autistic children are under and how we have to find a way to help them avoid the turbulence they are pulled toward as if to a magnet.

At this stage Steven's mother and I were both present during all his rides and he was showing good progress in the language department—he could name more and more objects during the rides, such as different trees and leaves. He would also notice and remark on ants, butterflies, or other insects—and animals—that he saw as we went through the woods.

September 2007

Steven went back to his daycare because his mother was expecting another baby.

October 2007

Steven was by now completely at ease on horseback. He loved galloping but was aware of the slight danger. He would put this recognition into words as indeed he was doing for all his emotions.

November 2007

One day, just when the session was drawing to a close, Steven ran up to his mother in tears. I never interfered when this happened and left his mother to console him. I just said, as they were leaving, "Mom will look after you, Steven. I'll be seeing you later." When Steven next appeared he was absolutely radiant with good humor. I said to him, with a smile, "I can see you are happy," and thereafter, whenever I smiled he said, "Happy!"

December 2007

Steven was going through another phase of overturning the props we use in the arena. He would look at me with a smile as if he were testing how far he could push me. At first, I picked them up without saying anything but finally, it became rather annoying, so I asked him to dismount and help restore order, which he did willingly, but looked at me and said, "Naughty!" I replied, "I'm a bit upset with you!" Given the progress we were making at the time, I considered it safe to express discontent as well as pleasure. Nicolas de Lahaye made a comment about this, saying that it is fine to display happiness or annoyance as long as they are truthful emotions. Autistic children can distinguish between the real thing and when you are putting it on.

When I am dealing with Steven's changes of mood I make sure to use my body language to reinforce my reactions, as well as the expressions on my face and the tone of my voice. By this time we had progressed beyond the primitive early stages; without frightening him, I wanted to display emotions that were an appropriate response to those he displayed. We were, after all, on the threshold of a really significant and beautiful relationship that brought me profound pleasure.

February 2008

Steven's little brother Alex was born this month. Steven rang me to tell me himself. Stephanie said, when she saw me, that Steven was very attentive to Alex and appeared to feel he was his protector. In the meantime, Steven's father accompanied him to the pony club when business allowed.

April 2008

Steven showed signs of being jealous of his new brother.

August 2008

Steven was making good linguistic advances. He had lots to stimulate him at home, doing puzzles, looking at pictures in books and naming all the contents that he could see, and he knew all his colors. He was particularly taken with certain comics and intrigued by cars and races. Altogether, he was settling down in life and appeared calmer on the outside.

September 2008

Back at daycare, Steven was put in the company of very young children about three years old, and he began to regress. Once again, he was wetting and messing his pants. Apparently the children, not infrequently, hit him. When he came to me, he made clear his fear and even began to cry again. At the slightest unaccustomed noise he would cover his ears with his hands.

October 2008

Steven's family and his doctor suggested that instead of daycare, the boy be sent as an outpatient to the hospital where I work part time.

February 2008

One day Nicolas de Lahaye came to join Steven and me on one of our excursions in the woods. He reminded me that it was two years since he had accompanied us. I stood on one side of the pony and Nicolas on the other as Steven was helped into the saddle. Steven, by the way, was now four years old. Suddenly Steven put out his arm to embrace Nicolas, who told me later that this action made him think of the baby who attaches himself to his mother at the age or stage when there is not yet a proper demarcation between the interior and exterior world. Rosella Sandri says, "Trying to glue himself to another person means that the separate existence of the other person is still not recognized."

Autistic children are very good at choosing the right moment to attach themselves to someone when the other person is least expecting it. The action is a kind of intrusion into the other person's space, but it is important that the adult does not reject the action. The child needs closeness and any rejection would damage their relationship. Nicolas de Lahaye saw Steven two years apart and immediately saw that the boy now recognized that he and Nicolas were two separate, distinct people. It was a notable advance. He also noticed that Steven's posture had improved and that he was altogether more confident and together.

That very afternoon, snow began to fall, and Nicolas noticed Steven sweeping the sky with his eyes. The boy seemed a little confused, so Nicolas let some flakes fall on his hand and then showed them to Steven who attempted to touch a flake but saw, instead, that he had touched Nicolas' hand. He looked at Nicolas and said, "I saw you."

After Nicolas had witnessed Steven smiling and using mimicry, he observed that the boy's interior life was much better defined than when he had last seen him. He told me that Steven could now make the distinction between himself and another because I had turned his anxieties and confusion into good experiences. Steven now had no need of my psychic envelope of protection. He had "grown" his own.

On the same day that Steven said, "I saw you," to Nicolas, he dismounted, turned toward his mother, and gave her an affectionate hug. By now he enjoyed such a wonderfully close and loving relationship with her I felt they could, between them, overcome every difficulty.

His mother proudly showed me his favorite sweater that had a horse's head on the front and told me about his progress with speech, how he helped willingly in the house, how he liked playing—especially doing puzzles. The family was happy to respect the pace at which he was making these advances. They went along with it and kept me in touch all the time.

April 2009

One day Steven took down the nameplate above Balzamine's saddle—the pony he was about to ride. He pointed out the "B" and the "A" while at the same time saying, "Ba." His mother told me, as with the first words he spoke, that he was now speaking his first syllables and could recognize them in printed form. As so often previously, the pony club was a place of discovery and provided an environment that released his creativity. All learning can produce stress for autistic children but the pony club helps to reduce it to a minimum.

June 2009

Steven arrived on his father's shoulders giving me a rather angry look that I found hard to interpret. Once in the saddle he took off his right shoe and I had to put it on again. This mystery was solved at the following session when his mother told me that he had developed two plantar warts on his right foot.

During the afternoon we played the octopus game in which the children place colored rings on the appropriate tentacle: Steven performed correctly but all of a sudden, during the subsequent pause in the game, he began to cry quite loudly but without shedding any tears. His pony that is usually very calm also became agitated, so I went over to them and took them both under my wing. I got all the children to start walking their pony, and within moments, Steven and his pony were calm again. Steven gave me the feeling that he had disgorged something important and recovered his usual composure.

Although I made no attempt to put any meaning to what had taken place, it nevertheless gave me a certain amount of anxiety just watching Steven's distress. In fact, I had to take care not to transmit my own distress back to Steven. I had to get across to him that here was something he was capable of dealing with by himself. Just as I could, he had to see that he could contain the discomfort and cope with it.

I have learned how to deal with this kind of situation when working with my "baby riders." They also suffer sudden crises, often when they are separated from the parent or when the comforting movement of the pony stops. Steven's outburst came as a surprise, but it did not altogether throw me. I appreciated that Steven had needed to send me an urgent message:

this was his way of doing it. He was calling for help from another person, and of course I had to respond. During my work with Steven I had naturally got used to diverting his attention from his obsession of the moment to other objects and activities. I would often engage him in a game of throwing the balloon ball, and this particular game was an aid to encouraging eye contact. I could observe the direction of his eyes as the ball passed between us, and when his eyes met mine, it was always a satisfying and rewarding moment.

Victor

Knowing about my work with autistic children, a teacher-training institute sent Victor, a nine-year-old, to me for therapeutic riding one morning a week, and because of his very difficult behaviour, he was accompanied by two caregivers (I began this story on p. 139).

January 28, 2009

Victor arrived at the club and looked round the perimeter of the grounds, rather in the manner of a trapped prey looking for means of escape if required. To my surprise he jumped into the saddle of the pony I had prepared and we set off at a walk: Victor, me, and one of his caregivers. The rocking motion had the immediate effect of relaxing him, but he still looked straight in front of him, head on high and holding himself well, but paying no attention to either of us as though we did not exist.

February 4, 2009

Victor had no trouble in identifying, among a great many others, the helmet he had used on the first occasion, and also his pony's tack. Each one of his gestures told me he was looking at everything around him to see that all was in place. Whenever he noticed something that appeared to be in the wrong place, he stopped and stared hard at it. He never looked at me, but when I named various objects he repeated the name after me, so we were beginning to put some sort of relationship together. He understood the significance of the play objects around the arena and the games in which some of the objects were moved from one position to another; he took in the hanging objects and named them after I did.

February 25, 2009

At the end of February all of Paris was on vacation so I had a lot of adults at the center using the big arena at the same time that we were working in the smaller one. Victor suddenly pointed at the other children having a good time and was clearly happy at the sight, as indeed I was, too.

Later on, when he and I were the only people in the play area, I suggested a game in which we took advantage of all the props close to us: the big suspended balloon and the one on the ground, the balls that filled a bag by his side. He named the little circuit we were working in, "The Way of the Colors," and he really excelled at everything we did. He even tried a trot and was light and balanced in his saddle. Both his caregivers and I were very complimentary about his performance.

When the session was over, we accompanied a group of very young riders into the woods for an excursion, but when it was time to go back, Victor burst into tears, began to babble about Zorro, the fictional character, and began to wave his arms about angrily. I made the pony walk calmly along. I told him that he was on Zorro's horse—his pony happened to be jet black—and when he began to talk of monsters in the woods, I told him that he was a brave, strong knight and had nothing to fear. This worked until we got back to the arena when he again began to cry, gesticulating and shouting "Horrible babies," referring, no doubt, to the "baby riders" we had accompanied to the woods.

Instinctively, I took him in my arms and spoke to him like a baby. The two caregivers rushed up because Victor, quite unjustifiably in my opinion, had the reputation of being violent, but I had no problem. I whispered in his ear, "Victor, you're a nice baby and also a great horseman." I was grateful to the two caregivers who, while remaining close by, let me cope with Victor in my own way.

As he was leaving, I thought he needed to take with him something to connect to the pony club so I gave him a horse magazine. This worked for a time and he headed for the car, but then there was another crisis and I could understand why it needed several adults to hold him when he got really hysterical. Although he was not a great talker, he shouted, "Horrible babies!" again. This was followed by: "Calm down!" "Crocodiles!" And then, "Don't touch me! Take your hands off me!" It was a big contrast to his behavior while riding the pony.

March 4, 2009

Victor stroked his pony for the first time. Then he put his hands to his nose and sniffed them. Likewise in the forest he sniffed some of the pine branches that had a strong smell.

March 10, 2009

We were having some work done at the stables, so when I collected Victor's pony, I had to leave the rest of the herd in the paddock. They all tried to follow me because that is what usually happened, and when I prevented them, Victor's pony whinnied in order to call the others. Victor immediately stopped his ears with his fingers and showed signs of distress.

March 18, 2009

Victor had a look at the horses' mouth, and I could see that the teeth frightened him. He took my hand in his and moved it toward a pony's mouth as if to try and make me understand. In order to distract him while he was being mounted, I stood with my back toward the pony's head, and it seemed to me that this little incident had helped him to cross a hurdle. He relaxed and spoke about Zorro's horse. He even looked me in the eye at last.

March 24, 2009

I again let Victor ride one of the larger ponies that was black "like Zorro's horse." Meanwhile, Victor was talking better every time I saw him.

April 1, 2009

At the club Victor now followed me everywhere, and when he was fearful about doing something like fetching his pony in the paddock, he got me to do it in his place: I think he took me, at this stage, to be an extension of the pony. With Victor in the saddle, I led the pony toward others and stroked their muzzle on his behalf.

April 29, 2009

By this time I was including Victor in a group with other children. He watched them closely and I could see him imitating them. In subsequent sessions he completely accepted the others and interacted with them.

May 20, 2009

Victor actually took my hand and led me toward a pony so that I could caress its muzzle.

May 25, 2009

On this day we had eighty-one children, all of whom had some kind of problem, participating in equestrian games. It is something we do once every year together with the association for "Reeducation by Equitation," and with other specialist societies, children's nurseries, daycare, clinics, and mental health centers. Victor took part and seemed quite happy in this big, happy gathering of people, ponies, and horses.

At one point, I heard one of the teachers pointing Victor out to her companion, so I asked her if she knew him. She replied that she had looked after him at a children's nursery. One day he had looked at her fixedly and then spat in her eye. I could feel that she had been distressed by this and indeed, it is not uncommon for caregivers and teachers of children with autism to have disturbing experiences. I have had them myself. This book is part of my effort to help all the teachers and caregivers to look at potentially distressing incidents as events that make one stronger and more able to cope in the endlessly demanding task of helping these children.

Victor seemed quite liberated by the ambient joy of the day: he joined in all the games and was visibly happy, so much so that he let out little cries of pleasure from time to time and waved his arms. While I was walking with him, he pointed at a white pony, so I immediately put him in the saddle, and we walked about in this atmosphere that was strange to him, full of people, laughter, and activity. Whenever he was not next to me I could see that he was keeping an eye on my whereabouts, but he found time to caress the ponies and explore the arena. At the end of the day he proudly received a medal and was awarded a prize.

June 17, 2009

Victor brushed down his pony, taking great care to remove all the pieces of hay on its coat. He took part in a proper riding class and waited his turn calmly without any signs of frustration. He had learned how to wait and accept the delay.

June 24, 2009

I suggested to Victor that he ride a rather large white pony, and while it was being prepared, we fetched Victor's usual black pony in order to get it ready for his friend. Victor watched proceedings closely as I attached the black pony to a post. Suddenly, Victor began knocking his head against the wall. I put my arms around him and led him toward the white pony, saying, "Here you are, Victor. Here is your white pony ready for you." This had the effect of calming him down, and when he was safely in the saddle, he showed every sign of being especially proud of himself. What is more, he displayed his riding skills of turning, stopping, and trotting, though there was a moment when he was about to trot when he said, "I'm frightened." However, this was soon forgotten.

After six months with me Victor was beginning to talk. He repeated what was said but also spoke phrases in order to describe what he was thinking. Rather than explore only the perimeter of the pony club he went everywhere; he rode either white or black ponies without demur, and established a relationship with them. He became more aware of my true position in the pony club: he still needed me as a support when he was nervous about something and would, for instance, take my hand in his so that I "took his place" when it came time to brush down the pony or to touch its muzzle. I made use of this nervousness to show him that the pony was in no way dangerous and that we could together go through the fear barrier and find that everything was safe on the other side.

Although he could still lose his confidence and have an explosion, he improved a lot in six months, which truthfully is not a long time.

Conclusion

This book set out to tell you about a therapy that involves a physical activity based on riding ponies in a safe and controlled environment. The therapy is effective with babies and autistic children, and even adults. The experience awakens neural circuits that have not been developed until now, and it helps to close down those that are harmful or not wanted on the voyage. I treat every child as a unique individual; I observe him, I get to know him and I empathize with his distress. We move forward as one toward a brighter and safer future, and I help him to stand on his own feet. I set aside theories about the causes of autism and how to treat the problem; I learn to listen to each child's distress, and I often let him guide me in which approach we adopt.

Thanks to the ponies, I can help these children become aware of a viable life, free their body and their emotions from the chains of autism, and find happiness and fulfilment.

Much has been written about a person's psychic body envelope, the emotional "skin." It sends out and receives signals from the surrounding environment; it vibrates and resonates with what it contacts; and it contains all the experiences, both emotional and physical, that the person has lived through. An autistic person may have the idea of the envelope, but before he has learned to register any experiences, the envelope is more or less empty. Thanks to the pony, I can start the body envelope resonating and vibrating, and taking in experiences that are remembered. The psyche is given sustenance and the building blocks are put in place.

Autism is a condition in which fear of contact with the outside world, as well as auditory and visual problems, result from being starved of physical, emotional, and sensory nourishment. Those with autism find themselves in a circular hell in which they are trying to replace their lack of any meaningful relationship with desperate efforts to master their closed world.

When the pony arrives in their life, it stops the pointless circular movement that is leading nowhere, and it helps the child break out of this hopeless whirlpool by taking on his anxieties. I am there at the same time, listening to their suffering, playing the part of an intermediary, and responding to their signs of happiness by experiencing the same emotion. The children soon recognize this: Steven often looks at me and says, "Happy!"

The children's parents often try to diagnose the problems. They are themselves mired in incomprehension of what ails their kids. I give them all the support I can: I listen to them, I listen to the official authorities, but what matters to me is what the children themselves get across to me. It is they who show me the road to save them from their problems, and when they are in the saddle, these fine young riders bring new hope to the desperate parents.

The ponies not only enable the children to breach the enclosed world in which they exist but allow them first to gain an understanding of the pony itself and then of objects and people. Between the child, the parents, the pony, and myself, we build a new world that absorbs the parents' suffering, allows them to relax, gain in confidence, and join in the future of their fine young horseman that is opening out before them.

The end that we seek and that is essential for these children who have problems is to learn to exist in the real world and to cope with the unexpected without destroying themselves. The pony carries them, rocks them, favors the acceptance of physical contact, and understands their efforts at communication. It helps them build up an image of themselves by causing their posture to rectify itself, and it gives them free lessons in sensory awareness with its smells, sights, and sounds. It opens them to the real world.

In a parallel way to the growth of a "normal" baby, I set the scene for making a fresh start. Thanks to the rocking motion of the pony, the children in my program return to a point in their life that may be as early as the moment in which they were born. They can make a start at building their psychic body envelope at their own pace and in their own way. Some will make some steps toward being sociable, toward the pleasure of physical contact and movement. Others will make enough progress to enjoy a full and rewarding life, like the very young children who were entrusted to me by their parents and caregivers.

When I work with an autistic child, I watch like a hawk to see what interests him: the slightest flicker of interest shows me the way to go. An autistic adult can and does say occasionally "I like that," but little children may well be at the stage where they have not yet spoken an understandable word, so I have to pick up the necessary indications from their body language. Once we learn to laugh together, they invite me into their hitherto closed world from where we seek a way out by being aware of all the multiple sensations afforded us by the pony: smells, sounds, visual markers, tactile and proprioceptive stimuli. The autistic child in some way senses these stimuli without necessarily understanding them. I go along with this. I do not try to understand; I move along with them through the rooms of comprehension until we reach the entrance. It is his choice when to exit.

In a controlled, familiar, and safe environment, the child is exposed to group activities, to mimicry, to exchanged smiles, to objects of various shapes and sizes and if he is very fortunate, and we begin his reeducation soon enough—and this must almost certainly be younger than seven years of age—he can expect to lead a responsible and "normal" life.

Nevertheless, it must be said, if most regretfully, that autism tends toward a way of life that is more and more difficult to escape from. Sadly, the symptoms of autism are often ignored or swept under the rug as if ignoring them or pretending they are not there will make them go away.

Parents and caregivers must face the truth and not fail to recognize the symptoms at an early stage when it would be easier to achieve a new start. The sooner the better that symptoms are acknowledged—at an early stage, the symptoms are still plastic and malleable. As time passes, they become fixed. Fortunately the children that I have spoken about in this book were given to me soon after recognition of their problems, so they are all making steady progress. I do not deny that it is possible to make progress with adults who are autistic, but access to language, if not established in infancy, is no easy matter.

The current treatment of autistic children is not altogether satisfactory and our understanding of the condition is limited. We are navigating without radar. But what is clear to me is that these children have the need—like all other children—to be recognized, appreciated, and helped by other people so that they have a chance of putting themselves together and living a reasonable life. They are extremely sensitive to relationships and must therefore be treated as individual human beings and not as some object that must be reeducated. Delving down into their innermost recesses, discovering the early moment when things went haywire, and going forward from that point is a delicate undertaking, fraught with difficulty and bearing a huge responsibility. We, who try to help, are taking individuals who have protected themselves behind an iron curtain; we ask them to be vulnerable and to trust us as we guide them out of their impasse. These children have to trust us as they let us into their secret world, and take our hands as we guide them with love and understanding toward the light. Left alone, they cannot escape.

The pony, as I hope I have demonstrated, is the ideal companion in this task. Human beings are often in a hurry to achieve what they understand as required objectives. Ponies have no such ideas; they adapt easily to the child's rhythm. Humans are uneasy when they do not understand what is happening; the unknown makes them fearful so they attempt to systematize and dominate. They look for quantifiable results. For my part, I try to work without pressure; I refuse to train my ponies in the conventional way. Rather than relying on mindless repetition, I let the ponies and the children take their time. I watch to see at what speed they want to progress, and I believe this patience and lack of pressure allows them to rebuild their mental state in a way that could hardly be possible if there was pressure on them. Parents that have allowed their child to be "helped" by codified, hard and fast rules tell me of the disastrous results they often notice.

It was the ponies that really showed me the way, and I have used this knowledge to help my "baby riders" and then the autistic children. The methods I use with the two groups, as you have read, are not dissimilar.

All my experience and research with autistic children has led me to question my own ideas and beliefs in depth. I have grown to accept that they often have different perceptions from those we consider normal and try to impose on them. By trying to make them "normal," we have the effect of terrifying them even more than they already are. The only way, in my opinion, is to learn from them, listen to them, but not leave them in their parlous condition. Together with the pony I lead them out of the forest that is thick with dragons and every kind of unimaginable terror. I put aside the disagreements of the scientists who make studies of autism and very often come up with widely varying approaches to dealing with it.

For fifteen years Catherine Mathelin-Vanier and I have worked together to help these individuals, following our own convictions to help them escape their state. Therefore, I shall let Catherine conclude this book:

"My dream has been that the fortress in which these children hide themselves is perhaps not so invulnerable after all. My belief is that you have to find the password to let yourself in, and when you find it, the drawbridge lowers and you can cross over. The analyst has to learn to listen attentively so that he hears the magic word. These children are not from another planet as is so often implied by people who care for them; they are human beings like you and me, and we have to welcome them into our family."

The Next Step

By David Walser

was asked to translate this book by Trafalgar Square Books, and when
I finished the first draft, I decided to go to France to meet Claudine. I
found the experience of meeting her and seeing her at work electrify-
ing. She is clearly an exceptional person with very special gifts. What, of
course, one has to ask is: can a book describe what she does clearly enough
to be of some help to the reader? I hope with all my heart that it will.

Claudine has decided that it is the youngest children who are most in
need of help, and it is on them that she is now concentrating her energy. To
this end she has handed over the care and training of the older children—
from about seven years upward—to a colleague. Both groups include those
on the autism spectrum, and the rule applies that only one child with an
autism spectrum disorder is included in each riding session.

Luigi, who you have all met now, has moved onto the older group
because Claudine felt he was ready for the challenge, and as I watched
him galloping round the arena, a broad smile lighting up his face, I had
no doubt she was right. However, he still has a big step to take: agreeing
to start studying. So far he has resisted, but speaking to his grandfather, I
heard about his younger brother Edgardo, and how it is hoped that he will,
by his example, give his elder brother Luigi the urge to start.

As a child Edgardo also had his share of problems: for the first nine
months of his life he clung to his mother like a limpet. It was impossible

for her to do anything without holding him close to her. He was also what Claudine calls "closed in," the condition that shows up physically by a marked curving forward of the head and torso: forward and down. With the agreement of the parents, Claudine put him in a saddle and off they set.

The change that took place was swift and can only be called extraordinary. By the time Edgardo had been to three sessions, he was sitting up with a good posture and no longer insisted on clinging to his mother. He had taken the vitally important step toward independence and has never looked back. Exceptionally gifted when it comes to memory and ahead of his peers in many fields, the family are hoping that he will have the effect of triggering Luigi's interest in books and learning. His grandfather told me that Luigi has never shown any competitive spirit until recently. The brothers get on well, with no more mutual jealousy than one would expect with any pair of brothers, but until now, Luigi has been happy to let his younger brother take the lead. There are signs that this might be going to change!

Steven, on the other hand, has remained with Claudine because she feels that he is not quite ready for the move. As long as he is with younger children and mounted on the only large pony, he feels a certain importance; he feels special. When I was watching a session, Claudine put him in front so that he had to lead the group and the transitions from trot to canter. The problem was that with the almost unnatural ability to look behind him—as is apparently often the case with children who have autistic tendencies—he kept on turning his head around to look at all the others in the class following him, his face lit up by a large smile and keeping perfect balance.

Consequently, though, his pony would then drop the pace, leading to a little "pile-up" as the other children, barreling along on their ponies, caught up with him. A cheerful shout from Claudine soon had him breaking into a canter again and all was well—for a time.

When Claudine walked toward a small obstacle and shouted to Steven, "Like to do some jumping, Steven?" "No," he said quite firmly, but Claudine put the jump across the track and raised its single pole on two plastic standards. Steven could easily have avoided it as he led his little train around the perimeter, but not a bit of it. He glided over in a perfect jump, his body flexing and leaning forward like a seasoned rider, while some of the others followed suit.

One of these was Soline. Her proud father explained how it was only her third session and that, at first, she was terrified of the ponies. No sign of it now, as I could see. "Well done, Steven! You are a great rider!" shouted Claudine and his face became wreathed in smiles.

Once the walking, trotting, cantering, and jumping were over, we set off in a line of ponies and parents, with Claudine at the front, shouting encouragement to everyone. We headed for the wood of beech and oak, and the pine forest where the "dinosaurs and wolves live." A father told me that when his boy first became aware of the dinosaurs, he was frightened that they would come into his bedroom. He, the father, had solved the problem by making a notice that he pinned on the door, "No dinosaurs or wolves allowed." The problem vanished.

Steven still led the line, from time to time displaying this alarming ability to look directly behind him, but without in any way showing signs of being off balance. Later, on the walk, I asked a mother of a child without autism whether she thought it was a good thing for the children to be exposed to a child with ASD. "Certainly," she replied, "It just widens their perception of what is "normal." They do not see the autistic child as being different from them. When you see them all together, you often cannot tell who is autistic and who not. Claudine treats them all exactly the same and so they treat each other similarly."

I knew this would have delighted Claudine and it did so when I told her. I explained to her that in English we have no noun for an autistic person. "Autist" does not exist and I asked her whether she didn't think this better than the French label of "autiste." "Of course," she said. "I never use the term and hate it when the hospital psychiatrists and staff use it. When I protest they sound surprised and say, 'We have to have a term to describe each condition. What else can we do? There has to be a label!'

"I tell them these are not children with an illness. They are people who often have special qualities, including being highly sensitive and intelligent, but just with their own way of looking at the world. Their development has been arrested at an early stage and they have turned in on themselves, so we have to help them to come out of hiding and to allow their special gifts to flourish."

I had the feeling that Claudine would miss Steven terribly if he were to go to the older group, though I know she will welcome it when the time is right: he is so affectionate with her that on the first occasion that I met him, he rushed into her loving embrace, showering her with kisses and hugs while his mother and father looked on with appreciative smiles. When I told someone about this incident, they asked if the parents were ever jealous or "put out" by the closeness of Claudine's relationship with their child. I told her I had observed and spoken to a number of parents, and that the overwhelming impression I had received was one of delight and gratitude for the day when they met her, and for the transformation in their child.

I told Claudine about the question I had been asked and she confirmed that she never experienced any problem in this area. Anyone can see that she empathizes completely with the parents' problems and wishes to help them, perhaps even as much as she wants to help their child. She often speaks of their great suffering, particularly in the cases where the autism has not been properly diagnosed for many years or when the parents try to forget strange behavior, desperately hoping it will go away with advancing years.

I spoke to one parent who had been present when Steven spontaneously leaped off his pony during a canter without even the hint of a stagger, let alone falling. She was as impressed as Claudine had been: here was a child performing a highly skilled and athletic action, without any special training, who not long ago had been completely closed to the world.

At the bottom of the meadow where the ponies live, a new and impressive riding school is taking shape. On the occasion I was there, as soon as the day was ended and the ponies had been released into their pasture and wandered over to the protection of the trees, we trooped down to see the new building. The children were let loose in the fruit and vegetable garden that Claudine has planted at the side of the arena. They were soon busy amongst the inviting strawberries.

Margot, the cow that lives in the same field as the ponies and may well think she is one of them, followed us down until a fence prevented her going further. When we left, Margot followed us back to the other end of the meadow; the children all said goodbye to her and the ponies, and Margot trumpeted her accustomed, "Moo!"

We climbed a steepish path back to the pony club and Claudine explained to me how the steeper ground around the new building is important: "This helps to teach them the third dimension. They have to climb up paths and come down them, something autistic children have great fear about before they start riding." She has also laid out a straight stretch of path that runs along the top: in this way, children learn that not every path that goes straight up over a rise will necessarily plunge over a cliff as they have hitherto been convinced.

"When we make the move, I will have chickens, rabbits, and goats down there as well. I want to immerse the children in the beauties of nature. This is my way to help them face and meet challenges ahead and to get over their problems."

Claudine plans to call this new enterprise, "Le Jardin d'Eveille," which implies it's a garden to widen their experience, waken their appreciation of the joys of life, and help them get along with other people. When she says, "Is this not a better solution than spending more and more money on hospitals and group homes and ways of cooping these children up together?" Who could think she is mistaken?

Claudine's dream is taking shape, and I am convinced it will be a success. Will it become a wider dream? There are horse lovers in all countries and people of goodwill, so we can hope that this model might be copied in other lands. Then, there will be a brighter future for all our children.

Right: Many of the techniques Claudine uses with her "baby riders" have helped her students with ASD. "Baby rider" Jeanne Riviere is shown here, in the saddle at eleven months (with her dad Anthony at the ready).

Below: "Baby rider" Jeanne Riviere in the saddle at twenty-six months.

Left: (From right to left) Louis Piroux, one of Claudine's students featured in this book, with Claudine, translator David Walser, and Louis' brother Edgar in the pony pasture.

Below: Claudine's new riding school, which she dreams will help children with ASD discover and appreciate the joys of life—beginning on the back of a pony.

Right: (From right to left) Steven Bassaille, one of Claudine's autistic students featured in this book, with Claudine and his mother Stephanie.

Below Left: Translator David Walser looks on as Steven embraces Claudine.

Below Right: Steven and Claudine enjoy a foray into the woods, along with Claudine's other students and their parents.

Selected Bibliography

Ali, Sami. *L'espace imaginaire*. Gallimard, 2000.

Alles-Jardel, Monique. "Le jeu, mode d'expression du jeune enfant et facteur de son développement," ("Play: the way in which a child expresses himself and a key to his development.") extract from *Journal du Psychologue*, December 1996–January 1997.

André, Christophe and Légeron, Patrick. *La peur des autres*. Odile Jacob, 2003.

Anzieu, Didier: professor at the University Paris X Nanterre and member of the French Psychoanalytic Association. *The Skin Ego*. Yale University Press, 1989.

--------. *Le penser, du moi-peau au moi-pensant*. Dunod, 1994.

--------. *The Psychic Envelope*. Karnac Books, 1990.

Astington, Janet Wilde: Professor at the Institute of Child Study, University of Toronto. *The Child's Discovery of the Mind (Developing Child)*. Harvard University Press, 1994.

Bagot, Jean-Didier. *Information, sensation et perception*. Armand Colin, 1999.

Bailly, Laurent; Darques, Dominique; Preat, Geneviève. *Des messages archaiques à la communication verbale*. Éditions F.E.N.T.A.C. (Federation nationale de thérapies avec le cheval), collection "Thérapies avec le cheval," 2000.

Barrey, Jean-Claude. "Le communication de la biologie à l'éthologie," *Colloque sur l'autisme et hippothérapie à Charleroy*, 9 decembre, 1995.

--------. *Le cheval de dressage, les mécanismes biologiques permettnt d'obtenir la estualité souhaitée*, compte-rendu du séminaire de dressage à l'E.N.E., 22 fevrier 1997.

--------. *Bases éthologiques de la communication entre l'homme et le cheval*.

--------. *L'éthologie equine au service de la thérapie avec le cheval*, F.E.N.T.A.C. "Thérapies avec le cheval," 2000.

Barron, Judy and Barron, Sean. *There's a Boy in Here*. Future Horizons, 2002.

Ben Soussan, Patrick: child psychiatrist in Marseilles; Knibielher, Yvonne: historian and professor emeritus at the University of Provence; Lemay, Michel; Sanguet, Marcel. "Qui a peur du grand méchant loup?" *Le bébé et ses peurs*, Érès, 2001.

Bernis, Jeanne. *L'imagination, Que sais-je?* P.U.F, 1975.

Bion, W.R. *Elements of Psychoanalysis*. Karnac Books, 1984.

Boysson-Bardies, Bénédicte de: psycholinguist, director of research at CNRS (National Center for Scientific Research). *How Language Comes to Children: From Birth to Two Years*. MIT Press, 2001.

Bowlby, John: psychiatrist. *Attachment and Loss Series Vol 1: Attachment*. Basic Books, 1983.

Briggs, Andrews. *Un espace pour survivre*. Hublot, 2006.

Bullinger, André. *Le développement sensori-moteur de l'enfant et ses avatars*. Érès, 2007.

Changeux, Jean-Pierre. *Neuronal Man*. Princeton University Press, 1997.

Chemma, Roland and Vandermersch, Bernard. *Dictionnaire de la psychanalyse*. Larousse, 2003.

Chicaud, Marie-Bernard. *La confiance en soi*. Bayard, 2001.

Cohen-Solal, Julien: child psychiatrist and consultant to the Hôpitaux de Paris and Golse, Bernard: child psychiatrist and psychoanalyst. *Au début de la vie psychique*. Odile Jacob, 1999.

Courre, Brigitte: philosopher and expert in the field of state help for autistic children. (A.O.R.P.E, 2003).

Cyrulnik, Boris: neuropsychiatrist. *Mémoire de singe et paroles d'homme*. Hachette, Collection Pluriel, 1983.

‒‒‒‒‒‒‒‒‒. *Les villains petits canards*. Odile Jacob, 2001.

Damasio, Antonio R. *The Feeling of What Happens*. Mariner Books, 2000.

‒‒‒‒‒‒‒‒‒. *Descartes' Error: Emotion, Reason, and the Human Brain*. Penguin, 2005.

Delion, Pierre. *Les bébés à risqué autistique*. Érès, 2005.

Deldime, Roger and Vermeulen, Sonia. *Le développement de l'enfant*. De Boek & Belin, 1997.

Dolto, Françoise. *Au jeu du désir*. Le Seuil, 1981.

‒‒‒‒‒‒‒‒‒. *Tout est langage*. Gallimard, 1994.

‒‒‒‒‒‒‒‒‒. *L'enfant dans la ville*. Mercure de France, 1998.

‒‒‒‒‒‒‒‒‒. *Es étapes majeures de l'enfance*. Folio Essais, 1998.

Poney Club de France. *Équitation par le jeu*. Écho des Poneys, 1995.

Fraiberg, S.H. *The Magic Years: Understanding and Handling the Problems of Early Childhood*. Scribner, 1996.

Freud, Sigmund. *The Uncanny*. Penguin Classics, 2003.

Giordan, André. *Apprendre*. Belin, 1998.

Golse, Bernard. *Du corps à la pensée*. P.U.F. 2001.

‒‒‒‒‒‒‒‒‒ and Delion, Pierre. *Autisme: état des lieux et horizons*. Érès, 2005.

Grandin, Temple. *Thinking in Pictures*. Vintage, 1996, 2010.

Haddon, Mark. *The Curious Incident of the Dog in the Nighttime*. Vintage, 2004.

Hontang, Maurice. *La psychologie du cheval*. Centre d'étude et de promotion de la lecture. Petite Bibliothèque Payot, 1989.

Houzel, Dider. *L'aube de la vie psychique*. E.S. F. 2002.

‒‒‒‒‒‒‒‒‒. *Le concept d'enveloppe psychique*. In Press, 2005.

Isaacson, Rupert. *The Horse Boy: A Memoir of Healing*. Back Bay Books, 2010.

Jeannerod, Marc: professor at the University Claude-Bernard, Lyon I, and director of the Institute des Sciences Cognitives. *The Brain Machine: The Development of Neurophysiological Thought.* Harvard University Press, 1985.

Kniebielher, Yvonne. *Peurs de jadis, peurs de naguère.* Érès, 2001.

Lacan, Jacques. *The Mirror Stage (1937) collected in Ecrits, The First Complete Edition in English.* W.W. Norton, 2007.

Lafon, Robert. *Vocabulaire de psychopèdagogie et de psychiatre chez l'enfant.* P.U.F. 2006.

Lécuyer, Roger: professor of psychology at the Institute of Psychology, University Paris V. *Comprendre l'intelligence des bébés.* InterÉditions, 2002.

Ledoux, Michel-Henri. *Dictionnaire raisonné de l'oeuvre de Françoise Dolto.* Désir Payot, 2006.

Le Guerer, Annick. *À fleur de peau, corps, odeurs et parfums.* Belin, 2003.

Lemay, Michel. *L'éclosion psychique de l'être humain.* Flwurus, 1964.

--------. *L'autisme aujourd'hui.* Odile Jacob, 2004.

Lieberman, Alicia, F: professor in the Department of Psychiatry at University of California, San Francisco. *Emotional Life of the Todder.* Free Press, 1995.

Lubersac, Renée de. *Thérapies avec le cheval,* F.E.N.T.A.C.

Mahler, Margaret. *Infantile Psychosis and Early Contributions.* Jason Aronson, 1994.

Mathelin, Catherine. *Qu'est-ce qu'on a fair à Freud pour avoir des enfants pareils?* Denöel, 2000.

Meltzer, D; Bremner, S; Hoxter, S; Weddell, D; Wittenberg, I. *Explorations in Autism: A Psychoanalytic Study.* Karnac Books, 2008.

Michelet, André. *Les outils de l'enfance II.* Delachaux et Niestle, 1972.

Mijolla-Mellor, Sophie de. "La conscience de soi chez l'enfant." *Au début de la vie psychique.* Odile Jacob, 1999.

Montagner, Hubert. *L'enfant at l'animal—les emotions qui libèrent l'intelligence.* Odile Jacob, 2002.

--------. *L'arbre enfant.* Odle Jacob, 2006.

Montagu, Ashley. *Touching: The Human Significance of the Skin.* William Morrow, 1986.

Montessori, Méthode. *Esprit et technique.* Don Bosco éditeur, 2003.

Mottron, Laurent. *L'autisme: un autre intelligence.* Mardage, 2004.

Ollivier, Dominique. *La vérité sur l'équilibre.* Belin, 1999.

Peeters, Theo. *Autism: From Theoretical Understanding to Educational Intervention.* Singular Publishing Group, 1997.

Piaget, Jean. *The Origins of Intelligence in Children.* W.W. Norton, 1998.

--------. *The Construction of Reality in the Child.* Routledge, 1955.

----------. *Play, Dreams and Imitation in Childhood.* W.W. Norton, 1962.

Pierrehumbert, Blaise. *Le premier lien, théorie, de l'attachement.* Odile Jacob, 2002.

Picq, Pascal: paleontologist; Digard, Jean Pierre: ethnologist and director of research at CNRS; Cyrulnik, Boris; Matignon, Karine-Lou: journalist. *La plus belle histoire des animaux.* Le Seuil, 1999.

Preat, Geneviève. *Logopede-orthophoniste,* Thérapies avec le cheval F.E.N.T.A.C. 2000.

Ribas, Denys. *L'énigma des enfants autistes.* Pluriel, 2003.

Rousseau, Jean Jacques. *Emile, or On Education.* Brownell Press, 2007.

Sandra, Rosella. *La Maman et son bébé, un regard.* Césura Lyon, 2008.

Siaud-Facchin, Jeanne. *L'enfant surdoué.* Odile Jacob, 2002.

Sillamy, Norbert. *Dictionnaire de psychologie.* Larousse, 2003.

Sivadon, Paul and Gantheret, F. *La reeducation corporelle des fonctions mentales.* Collection Sciences Humaines Appliquées, E.S.A., 1969.

Spitz, René. *The First Year of Life.* New York International Universities Press, 1965.

Symington, Joan with Symington, Neville. *The Clinical Thinking of Wilfred Bion.* Routledge, 1996.

Tabary, J.-C. *Élments d'introduction à la psychanalyse.* Nathan, 1996.

Tammet, Daniel. *Born on a Blue Day.* Free Press, 2007.

Touati, Armand. *Créativités, conditions, processus, impacts.* Hommes et Perspectives, 1992.

Tustin, Frances. *Autistic States in Childen.* Routledge, 1992.

Vanier, Alain. *Éléments d'introduction à la psychanalyse.* Nathan, 1996.

Velman, Frans. *Haptonomie Science de l'affectivité.* P.U.F, Césura collection l'enfant, 2008.

Visier, Jean-Pierre. *Au début de la vie psychique.* Odile Jacob, 1999.

Wallon, Henri. *Les origins du caractère chez l'enfant.* Collection SUP, 1993.

Williams, Donna. *Nobody Nowhere: The Remarkable Autobiography of an Autistic Girl.* Jessica Kingsley Pubishing, 1998.

Winnicott, D.W. *Maturational Processes and the Facilitating Environment: Studies in the Theory of Emotional Development.* Hogarth, 1965; Karnac Books, 1996.

----------. *Through Pediatrics to Psychoanalysis.* Basic Books, 1975.

----------. *Playing and Reality.* Routledge, 2005.

----------. *The Fear of Breakdown.* International Journal of Psychoanalysis 61 (3):351-7, 1980.

Index